Comments by Readers About

# The U. S. Housing Crisis - Lessons Learned

I read your book last night. I'm incredibly impressed! It's a huge undertaking to present an enormous wealth of REALLY important and helpful information in a streamlined way…but you guys did it! And, I think your readers will really appreciate the genuine tone and straight-forward approach—life changing stuff. Great job! I see this book being distributed in high schools, colleges (law schools particularly—some lawyers are not great when it comes to financial matters), vocational schools, and the like. I hope you're aiming to reach the masses with this one—the subject matter is so salient right now, and this information is really resonating with people.

– Jennifer Manganello, Esq., University of California,
Hastings College of the Law

I just finished reading your book. Outstanding! I love the unique way it was written in PowerPoint format—original, straightforward, and easy to follow. The information the book contains, and how it is explained, makes it stand out. You do not allow the reader to blame others or make excuses about their financial situation. You tell them to look in the mirror, take responsibility, and you show them that money problems are not hopeless but fixable. The stock and real estate invest-ing sections are informative and easy to understand. You take the com-plexity out of stock market investing. You show real estate investors the pitfalls to avoid. Readers will especially benefit from how you compare and contrast real estate investing with the stock market and other investments — bonds, precious metals and cash.

It's evident the book was written from firsthand experience, making it truly authentic. I am impressed both by your credentials and your experience counseling over 2,000 homeowners in financial distress since 2007. This book cuts to the core of what people need to know and do to put their financial house in order. I highly recommend your book! Read it and you will substantially increase your financial I.Q.

– Dory Laramore, Certified Registered Tax Preparer, and author of
*Get Your Finances Right: The Foundation for Success*

"The U. S. Housing Crisis – Lessons Learned" is well written, concise and provides a wealth of financial advice for every American. What is truly unique about the book is that the authors, an attorney and an MBA in finance, experienced investors, have listened to and counseled over 2,000 homeowners in financial distress since 2007. They talked to a cross section of America—attorneys, teachers, judges, bankers, retirees, medical doctors, engineers, labor union members, dentists, realtors, pastors, police officers, nurses, government workers, business owners, active duty and retired military, even a few CPAs, economists, and financial planners.

The authors learned that the housing crisis did not discriminate. All of these people wanted the American dream. All wanted to achieve financial security; substantially all failed. The authors ask a number of profound questions. What are the lessons of the housing crisis? Why are savings rates in the United States so low? Why do so many retire on Social Security only? Why do so many mismanage their financial affairs? How do we put our financial house in order? What do we need to know and do to be financially secure?

To answer these questions, the authors give concise details about the financial dealings of others and relate them to issues facing Americans today. As a result, this book will be an easy read for people who find financial matters confusing or even frightening. The guidance and recommendations in this book will help many take charge of their financial futures and move forward with their lives.

If you are among the fortunate, that is, if you believe your financial house is in order, you will also benefit from reading this book. Understand the lessons of the housing crisis and fine tune your financial plan and money management skills. Understand the mistakes that so many made and continue to make. You will also obtain significant insight about financial advisers, as well as investment products sold or available in the U. S. I especially appreciated the insights on how important it is to work together as a family unit to discuss and manage financial affairs.

Recommendation: Read the book! Money management, financial planning, and wealth building are mandatory subjects not electives. I was so impressed I asked my adult daughters to read it. They did!

– Andrew J. Sussman, Esq., Partner,
RSR Law Group, San Diego, California

# THE U.S. HOUSING CRISIS LESSONS LEARNED

*Increase Your Financial I.Q.*

*Make Smart Money Decisions*

*Achieve Wealth & Financial Security*

**Gary M. Laturno, Esq.**

**Victoria K. Kuick, MBA/Finance**

*"Many people today do not make smart money decisions"*. San Diego bankruptcy attorney

ISBN: 149094687X

ISBN-13: 9781490946870

Library of Congress Control Number: 2012920886

CreateSpace Independent Publishing Platform

North Charleston, South Carolina

# TABLE OF CONTENTS

# PREFACE

Welcome! A little background about why Vikki and I wrote "The U. S. Housing Crisis – Lessons Learned". My law firm's lease came to an end in 2006, and after practicing law for over twenty years, I was tired of fighting battles. I was not going to sign another long-term lease. So, I stepped down and became "Of Counsel" to my law firm.

The stock and housing markets crashed shortly thereafter. With time on my hands, I became active in the San Diego County Bar Association. Heather Rosing, the bar's president, asked me to chair the bar's Community Service Committee. I connected with Myrna Pasqual, Esq., founder of the Housing Opportunities Collaborative, a 501 (c) (3) organization, and Vino Pajanor, Executive Director of the collaborative. Both Myrna and Vino give a great deal to our community; they are super stars. For approximately four years, I served as the liaison between the Housing Collaborative and the San Diego County Bar Association, recruiting over five hundred San Diego attorneys to counsel distressed homeowners at HOME clinics in San Diego.

The challenge: Attorneys typically practice in one area of the law. They do not necessarily know about foreclosure law, mortgages, loan modifications, short sales, tax issues, deficiencies, bankruptcy, buying and bailing, and the like. I was asked to organize seminars and teach continuing legal education classes at the San Diego County Bar Association, other local bar associations, military bases, and the San Diego County Law Library, among other venues.

As a result of teaching continuing legal education classes, my phone started to ring. Attorneys who attended my classes referred clients, friends, and colleagues to me for counsel. Many of the attorneys who attended my classes became clients.

Since 2007, I have talked to attorneys, teachers, judges, pastors, bankers, retirees, medical doctors, engineers, dentists, labor union members, realtors, housing counselors, PhDs, FBI agents, police officers, nurses, government workers, couples pending divorce, small business owners, active duty and retired military, even a few CPAs, economists, and financial planners. The housing crisis did not discriminate! We wrote this book *partly* to share what we learned after listening to this cross section of America—from wage earners at the bottom of the pay scale to people in the top 1 percent.

In the last five years I have had an opportunity to counsel over 2,000 homeowners in financial distress. My law practice evolved from resolving legal disputes to resolving *both* legal and financial disputes. The message sent to all who contacted us: *Money problems are fixable; America is a country of second chances for everyone.*

Another event occurred in June 2011 that is pertinent to my decision to write this book. Mark, my son, graduated from high school. He came to me and said, "Dad, I want you to teach me how to buy investment real estate and to invest in the stock market." Mark read several investment books. He also attended a class on personal finance for attorneys that Vikki and I taught at the San Diego County Law Library. At 19,

Mark is now invested in three low-cost index funds—a total U.S. stock market index fund, a total international stock market index fund, and a total U.S. bond market investment grade index fund. Mark's only regret is that he should have started earlier.

A few words about Vikki Kuick, my wife and business partner: When my dad met Vikki, he said, "Gary, she is smart and good looking too. Marry her!" Warren Buffet said, "The most important decision you make in life is who you marry." I agree!

Vikki's knowledge and insights on the financial issues that challenge Americans today are substantial. She has significant knowledge regarding the stock market and real estate, having invested in both for many years. See "About the Authors" for additional information regarding our education and experience.

I continue to speak regularly on these topics and would be happy to appear before your group or organization. Feel free to contact me! My email is *Gary@LandKRealty.com*. Vikki's: *Vikki@LandKRealty.com*.

# PART 1

## The American Experience 2000-2013

# 1. PEOPLE DON'T PLAN TO FAIL. THEY FAIL TO PLAN*

*"We are our own worst enemy"*. Cicero, Roman philosopher

*"The majority of retirees get two-thirds to all of their income from Social* Security*"*. *New York Times*

● I recently met with Frank (not his/her real name) who told me that his finances were in "shambles." He asked for my counsel to assist with his financial situation. Frank had been successful in business for many years and had excellent income, easily putting him in the top 10 percent of all Americans. His challenge: he had substantial debt including past taxes, alimony, child support, and credit cards. Like many, Frank had followed a high-end life style—owning luxury homes, driving luxury cars, and living beyond his means. After paying his creditors, he had little to live on each month. Frank's biggest concerns: Would he ever get out of debt? Would he ever be able to retire?

- Frank's situation is not unusual. We have listened to countless people in financial distress since 2007. Many appeared to have wealth, but when we peeled the onion and examined their financials, we learned they had little or no wealth and no financial security. *All that glitters isn't gold.* They shared common characteristics:

  o None thought about financial goals or objectives.

  o Most made random, undisciplined decisions when spending; many did not know where their money went.

  o Nobody used a monthly financial statement.

  o They bought houses, cars, and other big ticket items without thinking how the decision would impact other financial needs.

  o Substantially all lived beyond their means with debts greater than their assets.

  o Many lived a high end life style and appeared to be doing well.

  o Few had assets, savings, or investments. Those that did save or invest typically had little money saved or invested.

- Note the Center for Retirement Research and the Employee Benefit Research Institute report staggering facts about retirement savings in the United States:

  o Less than half of all private sector workers in the United States have any pension coverage in their current job.

  o Thirty percent with coverage reported less than $1,000 in investments.

  o Many workers move in and out of coverage and take their money with them.

- Writers at the *New York Times* and the *Wall Street Journal* commented:

  o "Most retirees are heavily dependent on Social Security, which currently pays a modest benefit, on average, of $1,265 a month. . . . Only the top fifth of seniors with incomes above $57,960 do not rely on Social Security as their largest source of income; most of them are still working". *The New York Times*, March 30, 2013.

  o "Seventy-five percent of Americans nearing retirement age in 2010 had less than $30,000 in their retirement accounts," Teresa Ghilarducci, *The New York Times*, July 21, 2012.

  o *"Sixty percent of all workers surveyed had less than $25,000 in savings and investments,"* Brett Arends, *Wall Street Journal*, October 2012.

- Recommended reading: "Our Financial Failings", Neil Irwin, *Washington Post*, May 5, 2006; "10 Facts about the Financial Condition of Americans", Business Insider.com; "Finances of the Average American" freemoneyfinance.com; "Retirement Security across Generations - Are Americans Prepared for Their Golden Years?" The PEW Charitable Trusts, pewstates.org.

- *But there is good news!* If you bought too much house or too much car, if you have been unable to put money aside for retirement, if you wonder if you will ever get out of debt or be able to retire, do not despair. Financial problems are fixable. You are like many people in America - your neighbor, cousin, co-workers, doctor, attorney, pastor, rabbi, among others. See Chapter 4 below, *"The Good News! Money Problems Are Fixable!"*

- Read on! You will enjoy the journey!

*Statement attributed to Charles Berkley, first librarian of Congress.

# 2. HOW DID WE GO ASTRAY?

*"We are the only generation in history to borrow large sums to buy consumer goods"*. ArrangeFinance.Blogspost.com

*"I think we are seeing the culmination of a gradual change in philosophy"*. Richard Steiner, senior staff attorney, Legal Aid Society of San Diego, Inc.

- When Vikki and I were kids there were no car leases. People used cash. Most lived within their means. Bankruptcies were rare. Mortgages were often paid off.

- Our parents and grandparents who experienced the Great Depression of the 1930s would never buy goods and services unless they had the money to pay for them. They also saved and invested. (See "What Gary's Parents Taught Him about Money" in the Appendices.)

- From the 1980s to the early 2000s, Americans started to live beyond their means. We bought expensive houses and cars and started to spend more than we earned. Few thought about financial planning or living within their means. Few distinguished between necessities and discretionary spending. Few thought about putting part of their earnings each month into an automatic investment plan.

- To say "No" and to resist the temptation for newer, faster, or fancier products being advertised became challenging for us. When is enough, enough?

- The crash of the stock market in 2008 combined with the housing crisis caused many to rethink what is important:

  ○ Many are starting to wonder when and if they can retire.

  ○ "Maybe we don't need our 3000 square-foot home, a new car, an expensive vacation, or all the adult toys".

- Trends may be moving in the opposite direction. Some now buy smaller, less expensive homes; more people are renting. Some are buying fuel-efficient cars, cutting up credit cards, spending less, and starting to save.

# 3. WHO IS TO BLAME?

*"The problem with personal finance is in our mirror"*. Dave Ramsey, host of the nationally syndicated Dave Ramsey Show

*"The average person today spends anywhere from 10 to 30% more than they earn"*. Peter Serrano, financial blogger at personalfinancemastery.com

- Many people want to blame the financial institutions—"It's their fault. We want to sue the bank!" (From a couple who took over one million dollars out of their house over twenty-five years and an attorney who had not paid his mortgage for over three years)

- "I do not have a financial gene." (From a judge, a Harvard Law School graduate, who could not pay his mortgage and was drowning in debt)

- "Why won't the bank work with us? Why won't the bank give us a loan modification? " (From many who had no ability to pay their mortgage) Examples of the people making this type of statement include the following:

○ Attorney who earned $5,000 in 2011 with $1 million in debt against his home.

○ Handyman who made $1,500 per month with $900,000 in debt against his home, who at one time owned the home free and clear.

● What is the lesson learned? Who is to blame? Correct answer: Forget about who is to blame. Chasing after and blaming the bank for giving you a bad loan will not solve your financial problems. Take responsibility for your situation. Look in the mirror! You are in charge of your destiny and can recover. You can put your financial house in order, build wealth, and achieve financial security.

# 4. THE GOOD NEWS! MONEY PROBLEMS ARE FIXABLE!

*"God helps them who help themselves"*. Benjamin Franklin, *Poor Richard's Almanac*

- Bad things happen in life. We lose our jobs, find ourselves separated or divorced, become disabled, or find that a wage earner in our home has passed away. We may realize that we are overextended and cannot pay our mortgage.

- The good news is money problems are fixable. You can put your financial house in order!

- At the first sign of financial distress, take action. Consult with competent counsel—a real estate, bankruptcy, or tax attorney; a CPA; a HUD certified housing counselor; or a financial adviser. You may also need to see a healthcare professional. Financial distress and depression often go hand in hand. To find an attorney, call the Lawyer Referral Service of your local bar association. To find a HUD-certified housing counselor, see www.hud.gov. But do not wait too long. See "The Bad News" below.

- Some of the options open to you may include one or more of the following:

  O Best option: live within your means and pay your creditors.

  O Negotiate and settle with creditors.

  O Loan modifications on both owner-occupied and investor homes.

  O Short sales (discussed in Part IV) and deeds-in-lieu (you deed or give the house back to the bank) on both owner-occupied and investment property.

  O Refinancing under government programs such as HARP 2 and conventional REFIs.

  O Bankruptcy: you may be able to discharge many or all debts in bankruptcy and avoid paying income tax on the discharged debt.

  O Foreclosure: I have talked to many people who were angry because they lost their home to foreclosure, wanting to sue the bank. All had been in serious default on their mortgages. "I want a mortgage litigation attorney", many have said to me. None, however, appeared to have any viable legal claims against their bank. After listening to them vent and asking follow up questions, my comment on occasion was: "It appears the bank may have done you a favor. You no longer own a home you could not afford." Typical reply: "I never thought about it that way. You may be right." Recommended reading: "How Lenders Can Help Forestall Foreclosures", Anya Martin, *Wall Street Journal*, June 13, 2013.

O Defaulting on your legal obligations: In 2012, according to *The Wall Street Journal,* Americans walked away from $585 billion in mortgages & credit cards and much of which was simply written off by the banks. But note there is a dark side to walking away from debt. See "The Taxable Downside of Debt Forgiveness", Jennifer Waters, *Wall Street Journal,* March 10, 2013. In addition, the lender may pursue legal claims against you. At the very least, the lender may contact you, make a demand for money and at the same time threaten to sue. Finally, your credit scores will take a hit. Recommendation: Before you default on any debt, consult competent legal counsel to fully understand your options.

# 5. THE BAD NEWS

*"A fool and his money are soon parted"*. George
Buchanan, Scottish historian and scholar, 1506-1582

- Many people in financial distress understand that they have
  options but are unable to make a decision. Fear, ignorance, even
  depression may be at the root of their inability to take action.
  Some lack financial acumen and do not understand how much
  house they can afford. The typical result in both cases: the home
  is lost to foreclosure.

- Many in financial distress fall victim to frauds and scams:

  ○ California leads the nation in foreclosure rescue scams
    including loan modifications and mass joinder law suits.

  ○ Red flags: Is the promise is too good to be true? *Does the
    scammer want up-front money?* The result: the victims lose
    their homes, as well as the money given to the scammer.

- Many credit repair companies prey on individuals in distress.
  Beware if they make claims such as: "Credit problems? No

problem!" "We can remove bankruptcies, judgments, liens, and bad loans from your credit file forever!" "We can erase your bad credit—100% guaranteed." "Create a new credit identity—legally."

○ The Federal Trade Commission (FTC) says: "Don't believe them. They're very likely signs of a scam". Indeed, attorneys at the nation's consumer protection agency say they've never seen a legitimate credit-repair operation making these claims.

○ The fact is there is no quick way to fix your credit. You can improve your credit report legitimately, but it takes time, a conscious effort, and sticking to a personal debt repayment plan. See www.ftc.gov.

● Some pursue legal action against their lender with unfortunate results. I have listened to hundreds of borrowers who hired counsel to sue their lender. All paid their attorneys significant amounts of money. None were happy with the outcome. I have talked to countless attorneys in California who filed claims on behalf of borrowers against lenders. I found one who obtained a truly favorable outcome—Kamala Harris, California Attorney General (See forty-nine attorneys general versus major banks—a $25 billion dollar settlement in 2012).

● Many borrowers do not understand the following:

○ A lender has the right to foreclose on your home if you do not pay your mortgage as agreed. Courts have little or no sympathy with borrowers who do not pay their mortgages.

○ A lender is not required to give a borrower a loan modification. The government guidelines on loan modifications on the

Treasury Department's website specify the lender is to make a business decision relative to loan modification requests. What is in the lender's best interest? Will the lender do better if they modify the loan? Or, will they do better if they take the house back either through a short sale or foreclosure? These are decisions the lender makes—not the borrower.

O  If you do not obtain a loan modification, you are probably living in a house you cannot afford. The good news is that you are no longer burdened by the property. Many borrowers feel substantial relief when the battle is over. They are now in a position to get a fresh start, put their financial house in order and move to a home they can afford.

● To avoid making unwise financial decisions, we recommend contacting a credible financial adviser at the first sign of financial stress. Confer with your CPA and a HUD-certified housing counselor. See www.hud.gov to find housing counselors in your city. A real estate and bankruptcy attorney may be appropriate as well. Some have experience assisting borrowers in financial distress and charge a reasonable consulting fee. Some are available pro bono at consumer clinics sponsored by charities or local bar associations.

● Also, do not overlook the servicer of your mortgage, but beware, the servicer is a debt collector who works for the investor who owns your loan, not you. The servicer may give you false information. They may say anything to get you to make a mortgage payment. Confer with a HUD certified housing counselor or attorney both before and after speaking with your loan servicer.

# 6. LESSONS LEARNED: HOUSES

## a. Biggest Mistakes

*"Housing prices do not always go up"*. Joe Nocera, *New York Times*

*"Many people buy houses they cannot afford"*.
Gary M. Laturno, Esq.

Few people consider or think about other financial needs when they buy a house. What we want is often bigger than our wallet, and after buying a house many find they are in financial distress. Here is a list of the biggest mistakes we have seen:

- Many bought houses they could not afford and/or used their homes as a piggy bank or ATM, taking equity from the property.

  O During the run-up on housing prices in the early 2000s, some spent 10 times their income or more on a house, eventually going into bankruptcy and/or losing their home to foreclosure.

○ "Equity extraction was responsible for around 80% of defaults among homeowners who purchased their homes before 2004, representing around 30% of all defaults between 2006 and 2009". "Study: How Using Homes as ATMs Fueled Foreclosures", Nick Timiraos, *Wall Street Journal*, May 28, 2013.

- When it comes to your overall happiness, "there are a lot of better things you could be putting your money toward" than real estate. "Homeownership, the Key to Happiness?" Michelle Higgins, *New York Times*, July 12, 2013, quoting Dr. Elizabeth Dunn, University of British Columbia. (Dr. Dunn and Michael Norton, Harvard Business School, are co-authors of "Happy Money: The Science of Smarter Spending".)

- We keep houses we cannot afford and fight living within our means. Many run down savings and retirement accounts – if they have them – and/or run up credit cards to maintain their life style and pay for their mortgages. The end result is often bankruptcy and foreclosure.

- We buy and keep rental properties with significant negative cash flow. I have talked to many borrowers who spent thousands of dollars a year keeping a negative cash flow property. They took money out of savings or retirement accounts, borrowed money, or spent money they could have saved and invested. For example, a woman with whom I spoke contributed almost $40,000 over two years to pay HOA assessments and negative cash flow on her rental. With no savings left, she had to borrow $20,000 to pay medical bills. An active duty Army officer stationed abroad spent $60,000 over five years to pay the negative cash flow on his San Diego rental, losing the opportunity to save and invest a significant sum of money.

- High-income earners with zero or minimal net worth buy luxury homes.

  ○ One of the biggest mistakes by attorneys, medical doctors, and other high-income earners—those in the top 10 percent—is to buy luxury homes. I know! I have been there. I made that mistake. Money goes into the luxury home, and the owner typically has no money to save and invest.

  ○ Worst case and a not an uncommon situation: The owner's income falls; they have nothing to fall back on and lose their home.

  ○ So, avoid luxury homes unless you have substantial net worth. If you are a millionaire many times over with significant net worth, buy a luxury home. If not, forget it! A luxury home is a huge liability and may be a poor investment. See our discussion about houses in Parts 3 and 4.

  ○ In 2012, I spoke with an attorney who owed well over a million dollars on his house. In 2011, his income had fallen to five thousand dollars, and he had no savings and no ability to pay his mortgage. The man could not understand why his bank "would not work with him." Several months later he committed suicide.

  ○ A big lesson: Depression may result from financial problems. If you are in financial distress and "down in the dumps," contact your physician immediately. Talk to friends, family, and members of your support group. Call 911! Go to the nearest hospital! Do not wait! Depression is treatable!

- Few understand mortgages or basic mortgage information.

  ○ Few shop for loans with different lenders. It is not unusual for an individual or couple to look at dozens of houses, negotiate the price, and do significant due diligence before buying a property. These same people accept the first loan offered, giving up the opportunity to shop and compare fees and interest rates.

○ According to Zillow.com, one- quarter of all home buyers incorrectly believe they are obligated to close their loan with the lender who pre-approved them and that the best interest rates and fees can be found with the bank where they do business. "In fact, homebuyers should always shop multiple lenders to compare rates and fees to find the best loan". See "One – third of Homebuyers Surveyed Are Ill Prepared to Get a Mortgage", Zillow Press Release, May 10, 2013. Zillow.com

○ Many were sold negative amortization loans and subprime loans with teaser rates that increase significantly in a few years. With a negative amortization loan, the borrower has the option of paying less than the interest that accrues on the loan each month. The result: the debt or amount owed increases over time – not a good thing.

○ Some continue to pick adjustable rate mortgages (ARMs). With an ARM, payments change over time - going up or down to reflect interest rate movements. While this is beneficial if rates fall, it is unfortunate if rates rise. With a fixed rate loan, the payment remains the same over the term of the loan, and you can plan accordingly.

● We co-sign mortgages for our kids, other relatives and sometimes our friends. Bad idea! You are now responsible for the debt! If you are tempted to co-sign a mortgage, read "Co-Signing on the Dotted Line" by Vickie Elmer, *The New York Times,*

August 4, 2011. If you are still tempted to co-sign a mortgage, talk to a real estate attorney to fully understand what you are getting yourself into. Read "What You Should Teach Your Kids about Money" in the appendices. If your adult children cannot afford a house, do not cosign for their mortgage. Gifting people money makes them financially inept.

- People with little or no savings or investments put significant money into their homes. According to the National Association of Realtors, remodeling projects yield a negative return on investment. A two- story addition, for example, on average costs $152,470 and yields a return of 65.4%. Home office remodels and sunroom additions recoup the smallest returns (43.6%). See Realtormag.realtor.org.

  ○ *Recommendation:* Except for paint and possibly carpet, think long and hard before taking on expensive remodeling projects, especially when you have no savings or investments.

  ○ *Recommendation:* Make decisions about spending on your home based on an overall financial plan. *Before putting significant money into your house, consider other financial goals and objectives.*

- I have seen families frustrated and even lose their home after the death of a spouse because the spouse who signed the mortgage failed to authorize the lender to speak to another individual.

  ○ Here is an example. Wife signs loan documents to purchase family home. Husband and wife then take title according to different options available under state law. Wife subsequently dies. Husband contacts lender to discuss the loan; lender refuses to talk to husband, stating he was not a signer on the loan and they have no authority to speak to him.

○ To avoid this situation, wife, while living, can give the lender authority to speak to the husband, her children, or another individual. To accomplish the above, call the lender; ask what they require. Typically, the lender will require the spouse who signed the mortgage to submit a document to them that includes the following: loan account number, property address, name of other person or persons authorized to speak with the lender, mortgage signer's name and signature, and possibly the social security number. Some lenders will have their own authorization to release information forms; you may find one on their web site on line.

○ After you submit this document, follow up with the lender. Ensure the authorization is on file; ensure that the bank will speak to the husband or other individual.

○ If the servicer of the loan changes, for example, if the loan servicing moves from Wells Fargo to Bank of America, resubmit another authorization to the new servicer.

○ Recommended reading: "The Talk You Didn't Have With Your Parents Could Cost You", Tara Siegel Bernard, *New York Times*, May 24, 2013; "Leaving Behind the Digital Keys to Financial Lives", Paul Sullivan, *New York Times*, May 24, 2013

● Finally and perhaps the biggest mistake: *Many Americans have no investments except their home, thinking their house will take care of them during retirement.* Big mistake! "If your home is your largest investment, you are in financial trouble". Robert Kiyosaki, author "Rich Dad Poor Dad".

○ If you are getting started in life, if you are in your middle years, whatever your age, *do not view your home as the foundation of personal finance.*

○ *Recommendation: Create a financial plan and diversify investments.* See Parts 2 and 3 below. In Part 2 see Chapters 1 and 2, "What is the Secret to Building Wealth" and "The 25-50-25 Plan". In Part 3 see Chapters 2 and 3, "Compare and Contrast Investment Options" and "Houses versus the Stock Market".

## b. What Percentage of Your Income Should Go to Your House?
*"When it comes to your mortgage, it is not what you can qualify for; it is what you can afford".* Fred Holsman, Production Manager, Guild Mortgage, San Diego, CA

- "The unfortunate truth in America is that 37.5% of home owners are spending over 30% of their gross income on their home mortgage. *This puts a lot of financial burden on these home owners and often leads to foreclosure."* Statistic Brain Research Institute, Rasmussen Reports, August 4, 2012 (Rasmussen Reports is an American polling and media company, Wikipedia).

- The Rasmussen data reveals – not surprisingly - that states with the highest percentage of owners spending 30% or more each month on their mortgages - California 52.2%, Nevada, 47.1% and Florida, 49.2% - had the highest risk of foreclosures and that states where a smaller percentage of owners spent 30% or more each month on their mortgage for the most part had a lower risk of foreclosures.

- Our experience in counseling distressed homeowners revealed that substantially all spent over 30% of their gross income each month on mortgages. Many had other debts such as second mortgages, credit cards and car loans. Few if any thought about what percentage of their income each month should go to a home. Few thought about other investments. The idea of a written financial plan did not enter their mind.

- *The lesson*: If you decide to buy a house, first put a written financial plan in place. Think about your overall financial goals and objectives. Pay off other debts and then think about buying a house. Factor in the costs of home ownership – taxes, maintenance, insurance, HOA dues and assessments. Ensure you have money left after paying for your house to save and invest, pay for necessities, and enjoy life.

- *Smart financial guideline*: *If you want to build wealth, spend no more than 20 to 25 percent of your net income on housing each month.* That is, spend no more than 20 to 25 percent of your net income on the mortgage, property taxes, HOA dues, insurance, maintenance, and the like. See Part 2, "Create a Written Financial Plan - Practice Sound Money Management" below for information on creating a financial plan, as well as the 20 to 25 percent housing guideline.

- Be especially careful about trading up to a more expensive home. See Part 3, in particular Chapters 2 "Compare and Contrast Investment Options" and Chapter 3 "Houses vs. the Stock Market" before you rush out and buy a luxury home. If your goal is to become financially secure, do not put all your money into a house. Ensure you diversify investments, and ensure your portfolio contains some stocks.

- Compare and contrast: Todd and Margaret (not their real names) live in the same entry-level home they purchased in San Diego thirty-five years ago. Over the years, they resisted realtors who encouraged them to "trade up" to a luxury home. They said "No" to lenders who encouraged them to use their home as a piggy bank. Instead, they paid off their home early, saved, retired young, and now travel the world.

- Warren Buffett lives in an entry-level house he bought in Omaha, Nebraska, fifty years ago. Buffett is our most successful investor. Is he telling us something?

## c. Should You Ask for a Loan Modification?

*"The bad news: you will lose your house. The good news: you will lose your house"*. Thomas D. Rutledge, San Diego consumer attorney

- I talk to people every day who are desperate to get a loan modification. Here is the problem. The Home Affordable Modification Program specifies that a borrower's payment on their first mortgage should be no more than 31 percent of their *gross* monthly income. But 31 percent of one's gross monthly income is a large mortgage payment. After factoring in other costs of ownership, such as maintenance, insurance, utilities, and HOA fees, the total cost for one's first mortgage could be 50 percent or more of a borrower's net income. If the borrower has additional debt, for example, a second mortgage, credit cards, car loans, and the like, they will likely default on their mortgage and lose their home.

- Few people who receive loan modifications have said they now feel their financial house is in order. Their many other debts are in place; they are unable to save and invest or set money aside for their children for college. Nothing has changed. They must continue to pay for "too much house".

- So, the bottom line: many/most loan mods – *unless they involve a substantial principal reduction* - continue to keep borrowers in financial distress, delaying the day the borrower must face the reality they are living in a house they cannot afford. Not surprisingly, defaults on modified loans have been high. Treasury Secretary Timothy Geithner was candid in saying that a goal of HAMP was to slow the rate of foreclosures, preventing home prices from falling more rapidly.

## d. Is Renting a Smarter Financial Decision?

*"I am a renter by choice".* Salmon Kahn, Founder, Khan Academy

*"Few understand how expensive it is to own a home".* Gary Laturno

*"Even if a low mortgage rate means you spend less each month than you did when renting, upkeep can drain a bank account faster than a leaking water heater".* Michelle Higgins, *New York Times*

- According to a 2012 study by two economists, renting in the United States has historically been more affordable than buying. "I was shocked at how often renters won!" Ken Johnson, economist, Florida International University. "Our findings show that financially, *if renters exercise disciplined investing over time,* they can be more successful in accumulating wealth than those who own a home." *Real Estate Economics; Lessons From Over 30 years of Buy versus Rent; Is the American Dream Always Wise?"* Ken Johnson and Eli Beracha, economist, East Carolina University

- "Unless you need the security blanket of owning, it is nearly always a better financial move to rent rather than buy." David Kaufman, attorney, financial writer, and chief compliance officer of West Court Capital Corporation, investment advisers

- What is the best decision for you? The answer depends on a number of factors, for example, the current housing market, the monthly cost to rent versus the mortgage, additional home ownership costs, how long you plan to stay in the home, and your personal financial situation, that is, can you afford the payment?. Also, consider the lost opportunity to invest any down payment money into another investment.

- *Questions*: If you chose to rent, will you invest any money saved? If not, a monthly mortgage payment will serve as a method of forced saving. But if you buy, will you have money available after paying the mortgage and other housing expenses to save and invest each month? Do you want to rely solely on your home for retirement? If your home is your only investment, how will you support yourself after your working years end?

- Recommended reading: "How to Know Whether it's Time to Buy a Home – Six Considerations for Those Weighing Whether to Rent or Buy" by Amy Hoak, *Wall Street Journal*, November 28, 2011.

- Zillow.com has an interactive tool to assist in determining the "breakeven horizon", that is, the time it takes for buying to become more financially advantageous than renting. To locate the Zillow interactive tool - which provides data for cities and ZIP code and neighborhood within cities - go to http://www.zillowblog.com/research/2013/05/06/2013-q1-breakeven-horizon-expanded-to-neighborhood-zip-codes/

- Rent vs. Buy – David's story: David (not his real name) rented luxury homes in San Diego for many years. Some believed he was "throwing his money away", but David saw it differently. His rent payment, he said, gave him the opportunity to live in a luxury home for a great deal less each month than owning the same home, and – *a key to his financial plan* - he faithfully invested the difference each month. David also explained that as a renter he saved in many other ways—no costs to buy or sell, no cost to obtain a mortgage, no maintenance or rehab costs, no real estate taxes, lower insurance costs, and the flexibility to move or downsize. As a renter he made no down payment, which he typically invested. His rental security deposit, he pointed out, was often equivalent to one month's rent, small potatoes compared to a down payment. So, for David, renting was the smarter financial decision: His cost to rent was less than his cost to buy, and he saved and invested the difference. He was not, he said, "throwing his money away by renting."

- Marcy and Antoine, a thirty-year-old couple, are deciding whether to rent or buy. Assume they are thinking about buying a $500,000 home requiring a $100,000 down payment versus a rental that would cost $500 less each month. How will they fare at the age of sixty, assuming they rent and invest both the $100,000 down payment and the $6,000 saved each year on the mortgage?

- If they were to invest the $100,000 in a total U. S. stock market low cost index fund, assuming an average annual increase of 10 percent, it would grow to $1,745,000 in thirty years – *minus* the expense ratio charged by the fund. (See comment below as to why I selected an average annual return of 10 percent.) $6,000 invested each year, assuming an average annual increase of 10 percent, would grow to $1,091,660 in thirty years. Total: $2,836,660.00 - minus the expense ratio of the fund.

- As the years pass, rents will increase, and at some point their rent each month could be greater than their monthly mortgage. *On the other hand*, ownership costs such as taxes, routine maintenance and HOA fees will go up.

- If Marcy and Antoine were to buy the home and pay off the mortgage, assuming a 3.5 percent average annual increase in the home's value, the $500,000 home would be worth $1,403,000 in thirty years - about half what they might have if they were to rent and invest, as in the above example. In addition, Marcy and

Antoine will have significant additional housing costs expenses as the years pass that would cut into their profits. For example, over a 30 year period, they may decide to add a pool, an additional room and the like, receiving a low rate of return on their investment, *cutting significantly into their profits.* So, whether you buy or rent and invest, you will encounter an "expense ratio".

- I used the 10 percent and 3.5 percent figures in the calculations because stocks and houses in the United States, over one hundred years, have averaged an annual increase of approximately 10 percent and 3.5 percent, respectively. *Note of course historical returns do not guarantee future results.* See our discussion on this topic in Part 3, Chapter 2 "Compare and Contrast Investment Options," Chapter 3 "Houses versus the Stock Market," and Chapter 10 "Eight Guidelines to Successful Investing" below. *Recommended reading*: "Why Home Prices Change (Or Don't)" Robert Shiller, *The New York Times*, April 13, 2013.

- *The mortgage interest deduction:* I occasionally hear people tout the mortgage interest deduction, stating that it allows them to buy and live in a more expensive home. I have yet to find anybody who sits down with a CPA to ensure they are making a smart financial decision when they make this comment and then buy a house. Low income tax payers who do not itemize deductions are unable to benefit from the deduction. High income earners often use the deduction as a rationalization to buy more house than they can afford. Recommended reading: "A Deduction Unevenly Used", Lisa Prevost, *New York Times*, May 16, 2013.

- Takeaway: Do not use the mortgage interest deduction as an excuse for spending too much on your house. Because the deduction encourages debt, banks, not home owners, may be the real beneficiaries of the deduction.

- *The IRS Code & the mortgage interest deduction:* The IRS Code allows for a home mortgage interest deduction with limitations. First, the taxpayer must elect to itemize deductions, and the total itemized deductions must exceed the standard deduction. Thus, low income tax payers get no benefit. Second, the deduction is limited to interest on debts secured by a principal residence or a second home. (Note many members of Congress own second homes near the District of Columbia and thus benefit from the deduction. Given that members of Congress can be expected to do what is in their best interest, the deduction, it would appear, is unlikely to go away.) Third, interest is deductible on the first $1 million of debt used for acquiring, constructing, or substantially improving the residence, or the first $100,000 of home equity debt. See IRS.Gov or Wikipedia for further details.

- *Recommended reading*: "It's Not Everyone's Time to Buy a Home", by Carl Richards, *New York Times*, July 22, 2013

- *Recommended viewing:* You Tube Video - *Renting vs. Buying a Home* by the Khan Academy, YouTube.com.

  O  A little background: The founder of the Khan Academy, Salmon Khan, has three degrees from the Massachusetts Institute of Technology: a BS in mathematics, a BS in electrical engineering and computer science, and an MS in computer science. In addition, he has an MBA from Harvard Business School.

  O  Khan has produced over 3500 video lessons on a wide variety of subjects, primarily math and science. He explains complex material in an interesting and understandable way. In 2012, *Time* magazine named Kahn one of the 100 most influential people in the world. Wikipedia.com.

O  Khan, a renter by choice, describes his "Renting vs. Buying a Home" video as "the single most important video that anyone can watch".

## e. Should I Pay Off My Mortgage?

*"If your home is your largest investment, you are in financial trouble".* Robert Kiyosaki, author, *Rich Dad Poor Dad*

●  When I teach classes on personal finance to attorneys, I am occasionally asked, "If I have extra funds to invest each month, should I use those funds to pay off my mortgage?" My reply: "Good question! Let's discuss your question at the end of the class. I want to hear your thoughts at that time".

●  At the end of the class, or in follow up conversations after class, the typical comment: "It's now clear. If I have no other investments, I should not put *all* my extra money into a house. I need to diversify investments and ensure that some of my overall investment portfolio is invested in financial holdings".

●  So, like the students in the class, after you look at *your* monthly income and expenses, ensure that you have money to save and invest each month. Questions: How will you allocate those funds? What is the right balance among stocks, bonds, real estate and other asset classes in your investment plan? How important is a free and clear house? During your working years? During your retirement?

●  For further discussion on this topic, see Parts 2 and 3 below. In particular, in Part 2 see chapters, "What is the Secret to Building Wealth?",

"The 25-50-25 Plan" and "Get Ready for a Longer Retirement". In Part 3 see chapters, "Compare and Contrast Investment Options" and "Houses vs. the Stock Market".

- Recommended reading: "Should I Pay off the Mortgage?" Andrea Coombes, *Wall Street Journal*, May 23, 2013

# 7. LESSONS LEARNED: BANKS

*"If you look to a bank or mortgage broker for guidance on how much to spend on a home loan, your financial problems may be just beginning".* Gary M. Laturno, Esq.

*"Bankers encourage people to borrow beyond their means, preying especially on those who are financially unsophisticated".* Joseph E. Stiglitz, American economist, professor at Columbia University and recipient of the Noble Prize in Economics in 2001

- Countless numbers are approved for mortgages they cannot afford. *"If the bank says I am qualified, I must be able to afford it,"* from a man who earned $75,000 a year and qualified for a mortgage of $750,000, ten times his income. Unfortunately, he was forced to file for bankruptcy and subsequently lost his home to foreclosure.

- The above example is not unusual. Many are approved for mortgages in the United States to buy homes they cannot afford. But you may ask: Have things now changed? When a consumer shops for a mortgage, will they be approved only for a mortgage they truly can afford? The answer is "No". See "Lessons Learned: FHA & VA Loans" below.

- Do not look to a bank, mortgage broker or any sales person for guidance on how much to borrow or spend on anything. Their business is to sell loans and make money - not look after your financial interests.

- *Smart financial move:* Before you buy a house, put a financial plan in place. How much should you spend each month on a house? Should you pay off other debt before buying the house? Are you investing in a 401(k) or IRA? When you talk to the bank, do not ask, "How much money can I borrow?" but *ask* yourself, *"How much should I borrow?*

# 8. LESSONS LEARNED: FHA & VA LOANS

Are consumers being set up to fail?

*"Consumers shouldn't be set up to fail with mortgages they can't afford. Our new Ability–to-Repay rule protects borrowers from the kinds of risky lending practices that resulted in so many families losing their homes"*. Richard Cordray, Director, Consumer Financial Protection Bureau

*"FHA's low down payments and high loan limits encourage people to buy more home than they can possibly afford. Arguably, FHA has now replaced Countrywide as the nation's largest subprime lender"*. Jeb Hensarlin, (R-TX), House Financial Services Committee Chair

● The Consumer Financial Protection Bureau (CFPB) was created by Congress to ensure that consumers who applied for home loans had the ability to repay the loans. Effective January 10, 2014, mortgage loans will be prohibited where a borrower's debt to income ratio (DTI) is more than 43% of gross monthly income *unless the loan is guaranteed by the government.* For further information, see the CFPB web site at consumerfinance. gov. Search for qualified mortgages and the ability to pay rule.

- *Borrower Beware:* In our experience few if any people are able to save and invest when their debt to income ratio is 43% of gross monthly income. *If the loan is guaranteed by the government, however, a borrower could be approved for a loan where their debt to income ratio is greater than 43%.* If a borrower obtained an FHA loan, for example, s/he could pay well over 50% of their net income each month on all debts including their mortgage. We are aware of a number of FHA loans in San Diego that were approved where the DTI was approximately 60% of the borrower's *gross* monthly income.

- *Beware of new home builders:* Some buyers prefer new homes. Here is the rub: Developers typically overlook buyers' credit and cash problems and lure them to more expensive homes. It is similar to going to a car dealer hoping to buy a good used car at a reasonable price but driving off the lot with a $50,000 shiny new SUV. How do developers overlook cash and credit problems and lure people to expensive homes? Answer: They use FHA and VA loans. See "Builders Fuel Home Sale Rise" by Robbie Whelan and Conor Dourgherty, *Wall Street Journal*, February 27, 2013.

- Not surprisingly, FHA in 2012 -2013 reported that one out of six FHA loans was in default. My bet: Few if any FHA borrowers save and invest with such high debt to income ratios. Recommended reading: "Tangled in Housing Bust, FHA Seeks a Hand" by Nick Timiraos, *The Wall Street Journal*, February 10, 2013; "FHA Losses Could Hit $115 Billion" by Nick Timiraos, WSJ, June 3, 2013.

- What is the situation with respect to VA loans? See Appendices K "VA Loan Guidelines," contributed by Ken Bates, Military Home Programs, Inc., San Diego, CA. Mr. Bates reports that VA loans, unlike FHA, have low default rates. "Without any tangible reason for this, the conclusion drawn by most observers is that borrowers using VA are more committed to seeing their obligations through to the end. In essence, it's a character and integrity issue military members live day in and day out manifesting itself in the lower default rate".

- I have talked to dozens of active duty military people since 2007. Many had VA loans and high debt to income ratios; none had any savings. When transferred to a new duty station, given additional expenses, some said they had no choice but to default on their VA home loans. After relocation, some attempted to rent their old home often with poor results including negative cash flow and problems with tenants. Property managers, they learned, did not solve their problems.

- Question: Should one subject to transfer every few years be buying houses? "Since many people are more mobile as they advance their careers, buying may not be the best choice," Stan Humphries, Zillow's chief economist. I agree. As one who has owned investment properties in different cities in California, I quickly learned that investment real estate is a local business opportunity and that your chances of success with rentals are best when you personally manage the investment. One retired officer said to me: "I learned the hard way. After twenty years on active duty, I finally realized that I should not be buying houses unless I could live in the same community for many years."

- *Make Smart Money Decisions:* Before you buy a house, ensure that you will be able to live in the community long term. Pay off other debts first. Do not spend more than 20 to 25% *of* net income on *housing* each month. When you buy a house, ensure that you will have money available to save and invest each month. *See* "Part 2, Sound Money Management & Financial Planning" for a discussion on how to create a financial plan.

- If you own or are thinking about owning rental properties, read Part 4 "Investing in Houses: Pros & Cons, Biggest Mistakes, and Guidelines for Investors", as well as Part 3, Chapter 2 "Compare and Contrast Investment Options" and Chapter 3 "Houses versus the Stock Market".

# 9. LESSONS LEARNED: CREDIT CARDS

*"Overspending can be an addiction like alcoholism, drug abuse or compulsive gambling"*. Sheri Stuart, financial educator, credit.org

*"By using credit cards, everyone will buy more than if using cash"*. Arrangefinance.blogspot.com

- As a kid growing up in St. Paul, Minnesota, I recall that my parents lived within their means, did not use credit cards, and were able to save and invest. My friends commented that the financial situation in their families was no different. If their parents did not have money, they did not spend money. (For anyone interested in the history of credit cards, see "The History of Credit Cards" by Ben Woolsey and Emily Starbuck Gerson, as well as "50 Years Later, Credit cards in the Fabric of American Life" by Connie Prater - both at creditcards.com.)

- Fast forward to today. Many now believe there are benefits to credit cards and that credit cards can be used with discretion. That may be true for some people. Among those we have counseled, however, many were unable to use credit cards responsibly. Many of these people shared one thing in common: They had purchased too much house and then looked to credit cards as a way to maintain their life style and in some cases to pay their mortgage.

- So, do not be fooled. Credit cards can cause problems for many. If you do not have the money to pay for something, do not buy it. Best rule to follow: *Avoid credit cards.*

- If you do use credit cards, consider the recommendations of arrangefinance.blogspot.com:

    1.) Use a credit card only for items included in your monthly budget. If the item is not in your budget, do not buy it on credit.

    2.) Pay off the card every month. Do not pay interest on credit card debt.

    3.) Destroy the card if you are unable to pay the monthly bill. Do not use it or another credit card again.

# 10. LESSONS LEARNED: CARS

*"What is the ultimate driving machine? It is a car owned
free and clear".* Lyle Laturno, retired teacher

*"Don't drive yourself to the poor house".* Taylor Larimore, financial
mentor and co-author of *The Bogleheads' Guide to Investing*

- Cars are a depreciating asset not a way to build wealth. Good news: cars now last 300,000 miles! You can buy a good used car for a great deal less than a new car. Bad news: many continue to buy new cars, paying an average of $450 per month over many years.

- Self-made millionaires pay cash for used cars and invest the money saved. Warren Buffet, America's most successful investor, and John Bogle, creator of the low cost index fund in the 1970s and founder of The Vanguard Group, both drive used cars.

- Worried about car maintenance costs? In reality, car maintenance for a seven-year-old car averages 5 percent of your monthly budget versus a new car which is 15 percent of your budget.

- Imagine what you could earn if you bought a good used car for cash and invested $450 each month for forty years?

  ○ Four hundred fifty dollars invested for forty years at 7 percent per annum would give you a little over $1.2 million dollars - minus the expense ratio.

  ○ Four hundred fifty dollars invested for forty years at 10 percent would give you almost $2.9 million dollars - minus the expense ratio.

- Recommended reading: "96 Month Car Loans Wreck Your Wallet" Jennifer Waters, *Market Watch, Wall Street Journal*, 4/12/1013

- For suggestions on transportation options other than cars see Part 2, Chapter 7, "Sound Money Management – *Trim the Fat*".

# PART 2

## Create a Written Financial Plan &

## Practice Sound Money Management

# 1. WHAT IS WEALTH? HOW DOES ONE BECOME WEALTHY?

*"All that glitters isn't gold"*. Aesop, ancient Greek storyteller

*"I found the road to wealth when I learned that a part of all I earn is mine to keep forever"*. George S. Clason, *Richest Man in Babylon*

- What is wealth? Answer: The true measure of wealth is a sense of financial security. Wealth is not what other people see. "Defining wealth by what you see can be very misleading", Brian Parker, financial planner. "I've found that Ferrari owners can struggle to make payments, and multimillionaires may choose to ride their bike to work". Brian Parker, as quoted by Andrea Coombes in the *Wall Street Journal in* "Mom and Money: Lessons I Wish She Had Taught Me", May 12, 2013.

- So, how do millionaires become millionaires? How do they become financially secure? *The Millionaire Next Door,* written by Stanley and Danko, published in 1996, has contributed to our understanding of who the rich are, what they do, where they shop, what cars they drive, how they invest, and what we need to do to become one.

- See also *The Millionaire Teacher* by Andrew Halliman, a good case study showing how a teacher with minimal income saved, invested, and achieved wealth and financial security.

- Most self-made millionaires did not start rich. They typically started with nothing. Eighty percent are first generation affluent. That is, their parents were not rich. Their wealth is not measured by what they earn but by how much they save and invest over time.

- Self-made millionaires have a financial plan to build wealth. The average millionaire invests 20 percent of their income each month.

- Self-made millionaires pursue their plan with zeal, control their spending, live below their means, and avoid debt.

- Self-made millionaires acquire assets that work for them, for example, financial holdings and positive cash-flow real estate.

- Millionaires also marry right. Warren Buffet: "The most important decision you make in life is who you marry."

- "The people who build wealth work for decades and abstain from buying the bigger house or the new car so they can contribute the maximum to their 401(k) or IRA. They defer gratification to build a nest egg to avoid becoming a burden on their kids or their fellow taxpayers". *Wall Street Journal,* 4/14/13

# 2. THE 25 – 50 – 25 PLAN*

*"To be successful, you need written goals"*. Tom
Lehman, highly successful professional golfer

*"If you do not have a plan for your money, then there are millions
of people who do"*. Robert Kiyosaki, author, *Rich Dad Poor Dad*

- Roger J. Brown, PhD, former instructor at the University of California, Irvine, and San Diego State University, taught his students that all successful companies articulate financial goals and objectives. All have a plan to make profits. All have a plan to take our money. "When you go out into the real world, spend 80 percent of your time trying to get people to give you money; or, prevent people from taking your money."

- All of us are constantly bombarded with messages from companies wanting our business and are our money. The lesson: *Run your family's finances like a business*. Articulate personal and family financial goals and objectives. Be guarded with your check book. Do not spend money or let people take your money unless it is a part of your written financial plan.

- Of critical importance: *Pay yourself first!* Save a minimum of 10 percent each month by automatic deduction into an investment or savings account. You will not miss 10 percent from your monthly pay. Better: Save and invest 20 to 25 percent or more each payday. Start by investing in your company 401(k). If you do not have the option of a company 401(k), open and invest in an IRA. Then open and contribute monthly to a taxable investment account. Reinvest all interest and dividends. Let your money compound and work for you. *Do not take the money out until you are ready to retire.* See Part 3, "Invest in Low Cost Index Funds".

- *Spend no more than 50 percent of your income on necessities.* Pay off debt. Provide for your family, give to church and charity. Maintain adequate insurance. "This list is surprisingly short: a place to live, utilities, medical care, insurance, transportation, and minimum payments on legal obligations." Elizabeth Warren, U. S. Senator, Harvard Law Professor, co-author, *All Your Worth*

- *Spend no more than 25 percent on discretionary purchases.* "Once you get must haves and wants in balance, you can start to save automatically. You can do it without breaking a sweat. No more worrying. Just a simple, automatic plan for saving a certain portion of your paycheck each month." Elizabeth Warren

*Recommended reading:* See *"All Your Worth"* by Elizabeth Warren and Amelia Warren Tyagi for their recommendations regarding this important topic. Another excellent book, a classic: *The Richest Man in Babylon, by* George S. Clason.

# 3. COMPARE AND CONTRAST: CHINA VS. THE UNITED STATES

*"Most Chinese, even if their monthly income is less than $100, still manage to save quite a bit of money"*. Hung Huang, Chinese television host, author and actress

*"95% of Americans need to learn to save better. Schools need to teach real life classes"*. Email to *The New York Times* signed "MD"

- In China, savings rates as a percentage of income are one- third.

  - *Take note: the Chinese save one third of what they earn each year!*

  - The Chinese family that makes $60K per year saves $20K per year.

  - Chinese buyers put a minimum down payment of 40 percent on a first home and 60 percent on a second home.

- In the United States, savings are typically low or zero, and many Americans are deeply in debt as well.

- Many nations aggressively encourage citizens to save. The U.S. government promotes mass consumption and easy credit. Our nation's habits may not change, but if you want to achieve wealth and financial security, you must live within your means and save and invest each month.

# 4. GET READY FOR A LONGER RETIREMENT

*"Retire based on your bank account not your birthday"*. Joe Hearn, VP, Teckmeyer Financial

*"Prepare for a mix of work and leisure"*. Marc Freedman, CEO, Encore.org, nonprofit promoting second careers

- Significant financial contributions starting at a young age are required to have adequate retirement income. *"People vastly underestimate how much money it takes to have a lifetime income"*. Steve Vernon, President, Research Fellow, the California Institute for Finance, California Lutheran University

- Assume you are twenty-five and your goal is to have one million dollars by the time you reach age sixty-five. How much do you need to save and invest each month to reach this number? Assume at twenty-five you have $5,000 invested in your retirement account and you expect an average annual return on your investment of 6 percent. A simple financial calculator will reveal the annual contribution needed to reach one million dollars at the target age of sixty-five. The answer: $6,129.23 or $511.00 per month.

- Note the expected rate of return is critical. If you expect an annual return of 10 percent, and obtain a return of 6 percent, you will be in trouble. Thus, for planning purposes, *assume a more conservative rate of return*. If you get a higher return, you will be thrilled. For example, if you invest $6,000 each year and obtain an annual return of 10 percent, you would have a retirement fund of $2,881,851.61 at age sixty-five. The expenses you pay to invest are also critical in terms of how much you are able to accumulate at retirement. See Part 3, "Invest in Low Cost Index Funds".

- If you do not have a financial calculator, that's okay. Go to Bloomberg.com/personal-finance/calculators/retirement.

- The Bloomberg calculator is easy to use. Put in the numbers requested—target amount, current age, expected retirement age, and expected annual rate of return. Push the "calculate" button.

- Assume the goal is to have five million dollars by the time you retire. Your current age is twenty-five and you expect to retire at sixty-five. How much will you need to save and invest each month to reach five million dollars? If your average annual return is 6 percent, you will need a monthly contribution of $2,664.58. If your average annual return is 10 percent, you will need a monthly contribution of $898.75. *Assume the more conservative return and invest accordingly.*

- Biggest problem: Most do not start to invest early enough and may need to save two to three times more than what they are currently setting aside. There are options to address a shortfall:

O Consult your employer and possibly increase pretax contributions to your retirement plan.

O If self-employed, increase contributions to your IRA to the maximum allowed by law. Start an IRA if you do not currently have one.

O Invest on your own. Open a taxable investment account and purchase low-cost index funds. Contribute by automatic deduction each month. See Part 3 "Invest in Low Cost Index Funds" below.

O Work longer: Retirement may not be an option or even desirable for some. For each additional year worked, you will not make deductions from your retirement accounts, and you can continue to save and invest. What do you love to do? Continue to do it.

O Consider an annuity and a reverse mortgage. See Appendices for a discussion concerning both options.

● Recommended reading: "How to Get to Retirement? Practice!" Carolyn T. Geer, *Wall Street Journal*, February 17, 2013; "Retirement Savings: How Much is Enough?" Andrea Coombes, *Market Watch, Wall Street Journal*, February 16, 2013; "How to know if you have enough to retire", Robert Powell, *Market Watch, Wall Street Journal, May 25, 2013;* "For Retirees, a Million Dollar Illusion", Jeff Sommer, *New York Times,* June 8, 2013; *"Suddenly, Retiree Nest Eggs Look More Fragile,* Jeff Sommer, *New York Times*, June 15, 2013; "Money for Life", a book by Steve Vernon, longtime designer of corporate retirement programs, available on amazon.com.

# 5. FINANCIAL PLANS THAT FAIL

*"The first defense is diversification"*. John Longo, investment strategist, MDE Group, Morristown, New Jersey

- Do not put all your money into one investment. Diversify! We have seen many focus their investment portfolio 100 percent on real estate and not invest in their company 401(k) or an IRA. We have seen some focus their entire investment portfolio on one stock or one private equity or business opportunity. Big mistake!

- We have seen some invest everything into their business or law practice, believing those entities will take care of them forever. Big mistake! See, for example, the 2012 character-driven documentary film, *The Queen of Versailles*, about David Siegel, founder of Westgate Resorts, a real estate and timeshare company. Siegel—hugely successful—lived like a king until the crash in 2008. Unable to get funding for the buyers of his timeshares, his company collapsed. Siegel had no plan B; he had no other investments. The film shows the fallout from his failure to consider the possibility that his business would be unsuccessful.

- "One study found that 40 percent of business owners had no retirement savings. For many reasons, saving for retirement is difficult for owners, but perhaps the biggest mistake many make is assuming that they do not need to save — that one day they will sell their businesses and live off the proceeds". "Sell a Business to Cover Retirement? Don't Count on it", Bryan Borzykowski, *New York Times*, July 24, 2013

- Be wary of investing in private equity opportunities or start-up companies that "cannot fail". I have listened to people who invested 100% of their money (or put a second mortgage on their home) in an enterprise that was going to make them rich. What happened? The enterprise failed. They lost their money or were stuck with a second mortgage on their house.

- Do not try to beat or time the stock market. The pros on Wall Street try and fail at this. See our discussion on this topic in Part 3 below.

- Be careful about flipping houses. If you do flips, ensure that you have a plan B. We have seen many try to flip houses and seen many fail. Costs to rehab may come in above budget, market conditions can change quickly, and prices may fall when you try to sell. Then the question: Do you have a plan B? Will you be able to rent the home with a positive cash flow and make a profit? If not, your financial problems may be just beginning.

- Do not buy investment property with negative cash flow hoping for appreciation. The plan will not work. You will lose money. See Part 1, Chapter 6, "Lessons Learned: Houses a. Biggest Mistakes" for examples of ordinary people who made this mistake.

- Lastly, be careful with self-directed IRAs. You can put almost any investment into a self-directed IRA. This fact does not make it a good investment. If you are thinking about putting an investment into your IRA, read Connor Dougherty's article, "Is That a Condo in Your IRA?", *The New York Times,* February 1, 2013.

# 6. SOUND MONEY MANAGEMENT – *GET STARTED*

*"Savvy money managers don't spend a lot of time looking for ways to save a few pennies. They charge right ahead to the big-ticket items, looking to make high-impact changes in the shortest period of time".*
Elizabeth Warren, U. S. Senator and former Harvard law professor

- What are your financial goals and timelines?

  ○ Retirement, an emergency fund, education, housing, travel, a vacation home, weddings?

  ○ What are your short, medium and long term goals?

  ○ What can you afford on a monthly basis to get you there?

- Audit your finances! Where does your money go?

  ○ Track all expenses for 30 days.

○ Use a pen and paper or an Excel spreadsheet. Know where every penny is going.

○ Consider asking your CPA or a fee based financial adviser to review your expenditures and give you his/her view of where your money goes. You might be surprised by what an objective observer sees that you do not. Note this person must represent you. S/he must be a fiduciary - not someone who sells financial products.

● In a relationship, open communication is vital.

○ Talk to your spouse or partner about money. Agree to disagree. Attempt to compromise. One may be a "saver" and the other a "spender." Every individual has personal feelings about money that may not change but can perhaps be refocused in the light of a larger financial plan or goal.

○ For additional information on couples and money, including suggestions on how to resolve financial disputes, see *"Couples Need More Than Love" below* in this chapter. Recommended reading: "Financial Opposites in a Life Together", Tara Siegel Bernard, *New York Times*, April 26, 2013.

● Talk to your kids about money; teach your kids about money. They need to understand what is realistic and in the family's best interest. Spending money you do not have is not in your best interest. It is not in your children's best interest. Do not keep them in the dark. Bring them into the family's inner circle. Teach them financial planning and sound money management. Send them into the world with skills that will benefit them a lifetime. See *"Teach Your Kids About Money"* in the Appendices.

# 7. SOUND MONEY MANAGEMENT – *TRIM THE FAT*

*"Write your budget down. Sometimes people don't really know what's coming in and what's going out. One new client had a $1500 monthly gap".* Jeanne Gibson Sullivan, Certified Financial Planner

- Focus on the big ticket items - houses & cars.

  O Warren Buffett, for example, still buys used cars

  O My friend David rented houses

- *Houses*: If you are like most Americans, your biggest expense will be your house. The key: you cannot spend a large percentage of your income each month on your house – whether for a mortgage or rent. You must have money each month to save and invest. See "The Millionaire Next Door" and "The Millionaire Teacher" for examples of people who spent a small percentage of their income on housing and as a result were able to save and invest.

- *Gary's story*: Twenty years ago I lived in a luxury home near the ocean in La Jolla, one of the most expensive neighborhoods in one of America's most expensive cities, San Diego, CA. Even though I could afford to make the monthly mortgage payment, I was unable to save and invest. I had purchased "too much" house and ignored what my parents had taught me about living modestly and saving and investing.

  ○ Several years after I purchased the home San Diego experienced a recession and my income fell. The amount that I had to pay for my home now exceeded 50% of my monthly income. In some months I had to borrow to pay the mortgage. I struggled and was depressed. I eventually realized that I had no choice but to downsize and sell the house.

  ○ I moved to a rental property, started over, and fortunately met Vikki. We purchased an entry level home, live a modest lifestyle and save and invest.

  ○ I learned the hard way: I could not achieve wealth by living in a luxury home overlooking the ocean in La Jolla. The secret to achieving wealth for me: live within my means, spend a small percentage of my income on a house and invest.

- *Cars*: Here are four options to consider:

  1.) *Buy a used car with cash; invest the money saved each month*. Recommended reading: "Dump Your Car Loan and Pay for Your Next Car with Cash" by Carrie Smith located at PTMoney.com.

  2.) *Use public transportation*. Some have given up their car, relying on public transportation. For example, an attorney in San Diego who lives in a neighborhood near downtown

San Diego dumped her car and now uses public transportation, saving $450 a month. A study released in early 2013 by the American Public Transportation Association and the National Association of Realtors revealed that homeowners who live near public transit save significantly on transportation costs. Homeowners in Boston saved an average of $351 each month; homeowners in San Francisco saved an average of $346 each month. *Takeaway*: Take advantage of inexpensive public transportation and *invest the money saved each month.*

3.) *Buy a scooter.* Large numbers of people use scooters to get around in European cities. My youngest daughter who lives in the South of France drives a Mini, and her husband uses a scooter. He explains the price of his scooter was a great deal less than a car, and both insurance and fuel for the scooter are significantly cheaper. Another big bonus: unlike a car, he can park his scooter anywhere.

4.) *Bike to work:* You do not have to be poverty stricken to use your bike to get around. My oldest daughter, an avid cyclist who lives and practices law in San Francisco, often rides her bike to work. It gets better: Brian Parker, a financial planner, reported to Andrea Coombes of the Wall Street Journal: "I've found that Ferrari owners can struggle to make payments, and multimillionaires may choose to ride their bike to work". See "Mom and Money: Lessons I Wish She Had Taught Me". Amdrea Coombes, *Wall Street Journal*, May 12, 2013.

- Look for other ways to free up funds to save and invest.

  ○ Impulse shopping, insurance, vacations, credit cards, using stamps rather than on line bill pay – the list goes on.

O Do you own expensive toys? I have talked to people who have no savings or investments, but they make significant payments each month on RVs and boats. In addition, their toys are expensive to maintain.

O Restaurants & alcohol: Are you eating out often at expensive restaurants? Drinking expensive wine? *Drinking is highly overrated!* Cut back or eliminate alcohol consumption. Save money (invest the money saved.), lose weight, sleep and feel better.

O Take your lunch to work. Learn to cook. Eat at home. Eat out less often. Save money, lose weight, and feel better.

O Cable and cell phone bills: Do you use all those minutes? Do you really watch all of those extra TV channels? Stop magazines you do not read. Reduce memberships.

O Do you mismanage your debt? Assuming 18% interest, it would take twenty- four years to pay off a $2,000 credit card balance making minimum payments. ConsumerReports.org

O A financial "tune-up" should be at an annual project to keep things in check.

# 8. SOUND MONEY MANAGEMENT – *MOVE FORWARD*

*"It is imperative that you spend less than you earn"*.
Hank Coleman, financial writer and blogger

*"Any rich person will tell you. It's not how much you make. It's how much you keep. Saving is the road to wealth creation"*. Elizabeth Warren, former Harvard law professor and U. S. Senator

- Kick start the process. Pick one short-term goal to get yourself started and create a sense of urgency about the importance of saving money. Use your tax return wisely.

- Establish an emergency/rainy day fund. Depending on your age and financial situation, it should be at least three to six months income.

- Focus on paying off debt. Pay off your high-interest credit cards first. Prioritize. Retails store cards are often one of the highest. Student loans typically are the lowest.

- Create separate savings accounts for short-term goals: A down payment on a house, money to buy a used car, a vacation and holiday expenses.

- Make smart, not impulsive, purchasing decisions. Buy only what you can afford and pay cash for it. Live within your means.

- Start to invest. Take advantage of "free money" in your employer's 401(K) or open an IRA.

- Open a 529 College Savings Plan for your kids. See Part 3, Chapter 6, "The 529 College Savings Pan & the ROTH".

- *Recommended reading*: "Seven Resolutions to Get Your nest Egg in Shape" by Anne Tergesen, *The Wall Street Journal*, January 14, 2013; "Best Way to Stick to a Budget", Rachael Louise Ensign, *Wall Street Journal,* June 10, 2013.

# 9. FINANCIAL PLANNING SOFTWARE VS. A SPREADSHEET

*"Taking the time to track and analyze your income and where it's going is a crucial element of managing your personal finances"*. Len Penzo, money blogger

- Set aside time on a regular basis – once a day or once a week - to review credit or debit card statements and receipts. Keep track of every penny you spend using software, a spreadsheet or paper and pen. You must do it.

- Mint.com is by far the most popular and well-known home money management software available today.

  O Mint brings all financial information into one place including savings, checking, investments, auto, and home.

  O Mint helps you know how much money is left for each of your budget categories.

- ○ Mint helps you save money by reviewing spending and making recommendations.

- Two excellent additional resources: (1) "The Best Way to Manage Your Money" by Ian Sherr, Wall Street Journal, August 27, 2012; and (2) Len Penzo's money blog; in particular see his article http://lenpenzo.com/blog/id14307-why-i-prefer-a-spreadsheet-to-track-expenses-manage-my-finances.html

# 10. COUPLES NEED MORE THAN LOVE

*"Couples who get educated about investing, set goals and understand their risk tolerance can increase their chances not only of being able to afford another honeymoon one day, but also of wanting to spend it with each other"*. Veronica Dagher, *Wall Street Journal*, July, 15, 2013

- Money problems are the number one reason why marriages fail. So, confront financial issues in your family! Talk about money early in your relationship. Find a like-minded partner. Responsible conversations about money are a sign of a healthy relationship.

- Disclose financial records, discuss financial goals, budget your spending, treat your money as our money, keep credit cards separate, don't split costs 50-50—split costs according to your income and ability to contribute. Above all, talk to your spouse.

## Mediate Money Disputes
- Consult with a financial mediator, family therapist, or financial adviser. The individual should be neutral and not represent either

party. The advisor will listen with empathy, typically ask questions, and encourage each party to express themselves.

- As a mediator for approximately 12 years, I see how helpful it is for parties to talk and share their views, concerns, frustrations, hopes, and dreams with a neutral third party. After understanding what each party is thinking, the neutral party can attempt to bring the parties together and give them guidance and direction.

- Try mediation; best case: you will save your relationship; worst case, you will learn a great deal. Learning to compromise on your view toward money may be the most critical, important step to a healthy relationship. *Recommended reading*: "Money Talk before Marriage - a Tip You Can't Disparage" by Stacey Vanek Smith, *New York Times*, March 13, 2013; "Investing Advice for Newlyweds" by Veronica Dagher, Wall Street Journal, July 5, 2013.

# 11. SECRETS TO SAVING

*"Nickname your savings accounts. . . . The key is to automatically funnel money into those accounts each month".* Liz Weston, LizWeston.com

- SmartCookies.com, a financial website, interviewed top money bloggers to discuss what prevents most people from getting ahead. "Let's be real—it is just not easy to save money, but there are proven methods one can use to get ahead." SmartCookies. com.

- Adam Baker—ManvsDebt.com: "Write down all of your spending by hand, immediately after you make a purchase. It might seem old school, especially with all of the tracking technology and apps available, but it's more tangible and makes a bigger behavioral impact if you have to stop and physically write down every purchase. Do it for 30 days."

- Carrie Rocha—PocketYourDollars.com: "Check your tax withholdings NOW. Sometimes we're of the bigger-is-better mindset where tax refunds are concerned. Some even expect upwards of

*$7,000* back at the end of the year; that is *$583 per month* you could be saving. Even a more modest tax refund of $3,000 is $250 per month that you could use towards your savings."

- Well Chen—WiseBread.com: "Start with one small goal each week. Don't set yourself up to fail; start with one small goal you can realistically complete and build confidence to move forward. One goal might be to open a savings account."

- Liz Weston—AskLizWeston.com: "Nickname your savings accounts. Each one of your savings goals should have its own savings account. It makes it easier, and frankly more fun to save. Have as many accounts as you want. The key is to automatically funnel money into those accounts each month."

- J.D. Roth—GetRichSlowly.com: "Practice conscious spending. Impulse spending is tricky; you think you're focused on your saving's goals, suddenly you're in line at the grocery store mindlessly buying five packs of gum and a cheesy gossip magazine. It's important to think not just about how much money you're trying to save, but *what* you're saving for. Chances are it's something you LOVE."

# 12. USE CREDIT WISELY

*"Pay bills on time; avoid debt; maintain good credit; buy modest vehicles; begin investing early"*. Rob Berger, founder of the personal finance blog, the Dough Roller

*"Don't use a credit repair company offering a quick fix for a fee. There is little the company can do that you can't do yourself free"*. Ann Carrns, *New York Times*

- Credit remains an important factor in your financial profile. Using credit wisely can boost your credit scores.

- Credit scoring systems are complex and somewhat of a secret but here are some tips.

  ○ Make small purchases and pay off the balance in total each month. Do not max out the available balance. Keep balances low relative to the available balance.

  ○ Do not close old, paid off credit cards. Your credit score will go down. The longer you have "established" credit, the higher your scores. Those cards also contribute to your maximum total available credit, which is another metric tracked by credit reporting agencies.

- Paying the minimum on credit cards each month will put you into a hole, a big hole.

  O Minimum: 2 percent or 4 percent; as you accumulate interest charges, interest compounds on both purchases *and the interest*.

  O Assuming 18% interest, it would take 24 years to pay off a $2,000 balance making minimum payments. ConsumerReports.com

  O Additional fees such as late fees and annual fees drive the cost of credit even higher.

- Monitor your credit. Go to AnnualCreditReport.com. In December 2012, the Federal Trade Commission issued a report revealing that one in five consumers have confirmed errors in their credit reports. So, check your reports regularly. See FTC.gov.

- Recommended reading: "12 Debt Myths That Trip Up Consumers" by Rachel Louise Ensign, *The Wall Street Journal*, February 25, 2013; "Fixing Your Error Ridden Credit Report" by Anna Maria Andriotis, *Market Watch, The Wall Street Journal*, February 11, 2013; "Tips for Disputing Credit Report Errors" by Ann Carrns, *New York Times,* March 4, 2013, and "When Bill Collectors Knock" by Karen Blumenthal, *The Wall Street Journal*, February 12, 2013; "Can Bad Credit Hurt a Job Search?" Jonnelle Marte, *Wall Street Journal*, June 14, 2013.

# 13. HOW WILL YOU PAY FOR MAJOR MILESTONES?

*"Nearly half of America does not have enough savings to cover three months of expenses"*. Bankrate.com

- Graduations, college, and weddings are wonderful but expensive. They need to be a part of your overall financial plan. We have seen people lose their home after paying the bill for their daughter's $50,000 wedding.

- Set out a clear picture about what you can or cannot afford in age appropriate language to your children.

- Start the conversations about expectations for college and weddings EARLY.

- When will your responsibility end? High school? College? Graduate school?

- Set out what you expect of your child as to any contributions needed by them for college. Will they need to get a summer job? Will they be expected to work during the school year?

- *Recommended reading*: "For Parents to Be, a Few Financial & Legal Tips" by Tara Siegel Bernard, *New York Times*, March 8, 2013

# 14. INSURANCE IS AN IMPORTANT PART OF YOUR PLAN

*"Don't be caught empty handed; cover yourself with cash reserves and insurance"*. Burton Malkiel, <u>professor</u> of <u>economics</u>, <u>Princeton</u>

- Most everyone needs protection against catastrophic financial events.

- Your mortgage company requires home owners insurance to protect its interests in your home. Do not let it lapse if you pay down the mortgage.

- An unforeseen illness or accident could ruin you financially. Medical insurance protects against potentially huge bills and financial disaster.

- Life insurance protects a family and spouse in the event of death. Term insurance is inexpensive and can be cheap if you are in good health. Whole life, which combines investing and insurance, is a great deal more expensive. Term insurance makes sense for most people. If you want more information, read "Whole Life or Term Insurance?" in the April 2, 2012, issue of *Smart Money*, a *Wall Street Journal* publication, wsj.com.

- Other insurance is appropriate as well:

- Disability insurance provides earned income in the event that a disability prevents you from working *or doing your specific job*. It provides paid sick leave, as well as short and long-term benefits. "In the US a disabling accident occurs on average once every second." Wikipedia.com

- "Long-term care insurance covers for care generally not covered by health insurance, Medicare, or Medicaid. Individuals who require long-term care are generally not sick in the traditional sense but are unable to perform basic life activities such as dressing, bathing, eating, toileting, getting in and out of a bed or a chair, and walking. About 60 percent of people over sixty-five require some type of long-term care during their lifetime. About 40 percent of those receiving long-term care today are between eighteen and sixty-four." Wikipedia.com; Recommended reading: "Beyond Long Term Care" by Kelly Greene, *The Wall Street Journal*, February 15, 2013, and "Can You Afford to Get Older?" by Ellen E. Schultz, *The Wall Street Journal*, March 8, 2013.

- Umbrella insurance refers to a liability policy that protects the assets and future income of the insured in addition to his/her primary policies. "For example, if the insured carries an auto insurance policy with liability limits of $500,000 and a homeowner's insurance policy with a limit of $300,000, then with a million dollar umbrella, the insured's limits become in effect,

$1,500,000 on an auto liability claim and $1,300,000 on a homeowners liability claim." Wikipedia.com

- *Recommended reading*: "Making Sense of Social Security and Medicare" by Jennifer Waters, *Wall Street Journal*, March 24, 2013.

# 15. HIGH INCOME EARNERS - *HOW WILL YOU SPEND YOUR MONEY?*

*"We're dealing with the top 2% of wealth in the country. . . .But their financial I.Q. doesn't come close to their overall smarts level"*. Dan Di Pietro, chairman, law firm group, Citi Private Bank, 40,000 lawyer clients, quoted in "Money Advice for Doctors and Lawyers" by Paul Sullivan, *The New York Times*, March 30, 2013

- High income earners - like everybody else - can be terrible money managers, often assuming their high earnings will go on forever. Those with earnings that go on for many years often live beyond their means. Larry King, for example, has reportedly filed for bankruptcy on three different occasions. It is not uncommon for famous, highly paid athletes to have debts greater than their assets and to file bankruptcy.

- Recommendation: Take advantage of high earnings to create wealth and financial security for yourself and your family. Invest

50 percent *or more* of your earnings each month through automatic deduction into an investment account.

○ If you earn $300,000 a year, invest $150,000 and live on $150,000. Even better: invest $200,000 and live on $100,000.

○ If both parties in a relationship earn a substantial salary, invest one salary and live on the other.

- Avoid luxury homes and luxury cars. Both will/may go down in value. Both, especially luxury homes, require substantial money to maintain. The least financially smart thing you can do is buy luxury homes and luxury cars that drain funds you could use to invest.

- Develop a financial plan. Diversify investments. Do not spend too much on financial advisers. Keep investment costs low. See Part 3, "Invest in Low Cost Index Funds" below.

# 16. SMART MOVE – *DELAY TAKING SOCIAL SECURITY BENEFITS*

*"Choosing when to take Social Security is a complicated decision and should not be taken without consulting a competent adviser"*. Larry Branton, Esq., certified specialist – taxation law, State Bar of CA

*"It makes sense for women, married couples and those with good health to wait longer for a bigger paycheck"*. David Blanchett, head of retirement research for financial research firm Morningstar

- The longer you wait to take social security, the greater your monthly benefit when you receive payments:

  O If you wait to age sixty-six, payments go up by 33 percent.

  O If you wait until seventy, benefits go up by at least 75 percent.

- So, waiting is the easiest way to obtain more coverage. Few take advantage of these options:

  O Currently, 46 percent begin claiming benefits at sixty-two, the first year they are eligible.

  O Less than 5 percent delay past the age of sixty-six.

- When you approach retirement age, factors to consider in your decision to collect social security include your health, family longevity, employment, and financial situation.

- Recommended reading: "Bolstering Your Benefits" by Kelly Green, *Wall Street Journal*, March 15, 2013

# 17. WHAT CAN WE LEARN FROM SOCIAL SECURITY?

*"The system is not intended as a substitute for private savings, pension plans, and insurance protection".*
President Dwight D. Eisenhower, January 14, 1954

- Social Security may be the most popular and successful government program in American history. What can we learn from it?

- Social Security is mandatory. If you are employed in the private sector, you must participate. Each payday, $113,700 of your income is subject to a 6.2% payroll tax which is automatically withheld from you paycheck. At retirement, you receive a monthly annuity intended to cover basic necessities – not a luxury lifestyle.

- Do you want to enjoy more than the Spartan existence that Social Security provides? You can! Emulate Social Security; adopt the following guidelines.

1.). *Pay yourself first.* Via auto deduction, put a % of your income into a diversified *your* investment portfolio each payday. The more you can put into your investment account each month the better.

2.) *Leave the money alone.* Let it grow and compound. Do not take withdrawals until you retire.

- Sounds simple! It is! Few, however, save and invest. Many spend more than they earn and then rely on Social Security, finding they live a Spartan existence in their golden years. As Cicero said, "We are our own worst enemy".

- For a guidelines and recommendations on how to invest, see Part 3 below.

- Recommended reading: "Social Security, Present & Future", The Editorial Board, *The New York Times*, March 30, 2013; "It's Never Too Soon To Start Planning Your Retirement", Tom Lauricella, *Wall Street Journal,* May 27, 2013.

# 18. DO NOT SABOTAGE YOUR RETIREMENT PLANS

*"The greatest single source of wealth is between your ears".* Brian Tracy, speaker who addresses more than 250,000 people each year

- Most retirees are concerned that an event beyond their control will derail their retirement plan, for example, a stock market crash or a major medical issue.

- The truth is "we are our own worst enemy". We damage our own plans! For example, some of us make expensive renovations to their homes, buy second homes, "loan" money to kids or contribute large amounts to charities.

- When you think about doing anything that departs from your retirement plan, first consult a trusted fiduciary to review your plan and advise you accordingly.

- You have the ability to make the plan work well or poorly. Think long and hard before you make major changes in the plan except to increase monthly contributions.

# 19. HOW TO MAKE MORE MONEY

*"Even if money can't buy happiness, it's a pretty good start"*. David Weidner, *Wall Street Journal*

● Graduate from college!

○ "In 2012, the typical full-time worker with a bachelor's degree earned 79 percent more than a similar full-time worker with no more than a high school diploma. For comparison, 20 years earlier the premium was 73 percent, and 30 years earlier it was 48 percent". Catherine Rampell, *New York Times*.

○ Ms. Rampell: Students who borrow to attend college graduate with an average debt of $27,000, but their return on investment is high. According to the Hamilton Project of the Brookings Institution, the benefits of a four-year degree were equivalent to an investment that returns 15.2 percent per year, factoring in earnings students forgo while in school.

○ The Hamilton Project: "This is more than double the average return of stock market investments since 1950 and more than five times the returns of corporate bonds, gold, long-term government bonds, or homeownership". See "College Graduates Fare Well in Jobs Market", *New York Times*, May 3, 2013, Catherine Rampell.

● Exercise! Workers who exercise regularly earn nine percent more than those who do not. *Wall Street Journal*, June 2012

○ Walk, run, dance, lift weights, swim, ride a bike, work with a personal trainer. Result? Earn more money!

○ Why? Endorphins flow from exercise. Exercise makes us more effective in everything we do. Our mood improves. Our mind focuses better. We feel good about ourselves; we get sick less often. The quality of our life goes up.

● Grow up in the right city! A joint Harvard and University of California study finds the odds of rising to another income level are notably low in certain cities, for example, Atlanta and Charlotte, and much higher in other cities such as New York and Boston. See "In Climbing Income Ladder, Location Matters", by David Leonhardt, *New York Times*, July 22, 2013.

● What else can you do to increase your earnings?

○ Work multiple jobs. Go to graduate school. Get additional vocational training to enhance your skill set.

○ But be careful: Borrowing substantial sums to prepare for a job in a low-paying vocation or profession may be financially unwise. Some young people today have student loans in excess of $200,000 after leaving graduate or law school. After graduation, many tragically learn they are unable to find work. So, be careful about where you go to school and what you study.

○ *Recommended reading:* "A Smart Investor Would Skip the M. B. A." Dale Stephens, Wall Street Journal, March 1, 2013

# 20. STAY HEALTHY – MINIMIZE HEALTH CARE COSTS

*"Life is a one- time gift".* Author unknown

- "One of the best things you can do for retirement is to keep your-self in good health. Medical bills will be a great deal less; you'll take fewer trips to the emergency room, and most importantly, you'll feel better." Henry Hebler, Market Watch, *Wall Street Journal*, December 6, 2012

- "Fidelity, one of the largest holders of retirement accounts, estimates that a couple retiring at age 65 will spend $240,000 in 2012 dollars for health expenses the rest of their lives. This includes premiums and uninsured medical costs but does not include over-the-counter drugs, dental costs, and long-term care. Such numbers aren't in Fidelity's $240,000." Henry Hebler

- A question not answered by Hebler: How can one maintain good health and keep health care costs down? "Easier said than done", you say. Isn't heart disease, high blood pressure, diabetes, dementia, even cancer, among others, a natural consequence of aging? Science has answered these questions. The research - countless studies conducted at universities throughout the world over the last twenty years - reveals that a plant-based diet – vegetables, fruit, beans, seeds, and nuts - prevents and can even reverse degenerative disease. See "The China Study" by T. Colin Campbell, PhD, and Thomas M. Campbell II, MD, available at amazon.com.

- T. Colin Campbell, PhD, professor emeritus at Cornell, has spent the last forty five years studying the relationship between diet and disease in both animals and humans. "The China Study", an Oxford, Cornell and the University of Beijing project directed by Dr. Campbell, may be the most comprehensive study on the relationship between diet and disease ever conducted. The study's findings: *Degenerative disease is not a natural consequence of aging. A diet based on plants prevents and can reverse degenerative diseases.* See almost 2,000 reader reviews at amanzon.com/books.

- Also recommended: "Eat to Live" and "Super Immunity" by Joel Fuhrman, MD. Dr. Fuhrman, a board certified physician, has spent the last twenty years using a plant based diet to treat patients. Dr. Fuhrman has lectured on PBS; a DVD of his lectures may be available from your local PBS station. See reader reviews of his books at amazon.com/books.

- *A look at history*: 2,500 years ago Socrates, a founder of Western philosophy, wrote that doctors become needed and the "norm" in urban areas, given the way people eat and live in cities. Plato, student of Socrates and one of the greatest intellectuals in the history of the Western world, condemned meat eating. "We eat animals at our own peril", he wrote. Hippocrates, the father of Western medicine, advocated diet as the chief way to prevent *and* treat disease. See Williams Howard, *The Ethics of Diet. A Catena of Authorities Deprecatory of the Practice of Flesh-Eating,* London, F. Pitman, 1843

- *Gary's story*: I have always tried to exercise, keep my weight down, eat well, and I have enjoyed good health all my life. About five months ago, while visiting my doctor at Kaiser, he informed me that my blood pressure was elevated – a systolic of 150! He prescribed medication. "Is there another option?" I asked. "It's just a natural consequence of aging," he said. I did not accept his answer and went to the Kaiser web site to find a doctor for a second opinion. To my surprise, I found a doctor who advocated a plant based diet. He commented he "walked the talk", emphasizing fruit, vegetables and beans in his diet. So, I made an appointment to see him and also read "The China Study" and "Eat to Live" cited above. I quickly moved to a diet that substantially emphasized plants. After five months, my weight dropped from 178 to 164; my total blood cholesterol dropped from 220 to 156, and my blood pressure is now 114 over 75. I love this diet, sleep better, and feel great. My new doctor does not believe that degenerative disease as "a natural consequence of aging". My goal: maintain good health and enjoy my family, travel, golf, law practice, writing, and lecturing for many more years to come.

# 21. MARRIED COUPLE DISCUSS FINANCIAL PLANNING & MONEY MANAGEMENT

*"Articulate your financial goals. Track monthly income and expenses. Do not carry credit card balances. Pay cash for modest vehicles. Dump your luxury home. Save and invest each month"*. Michael & Andrea

- Gary met Michael, an attorney, in approximately 2003–2004, in San Diego and they stayed in touch.

- Several years later Michael met Andrea, a civil engineer, and the couple married. Both are bright, well educated, and have good paying jobs.

- Shortly after getting married they purchased a luxury home in San Diego for $800,000. We were surprised. Why did they buy such an expensive home? Would they be able to save and invest after paying their mortgage each month?

- In early 2012, the couple contacted us and said they wanted to sell their luxury home and downsize. They explained that they had high-stress jobs and did not want to work forever. They had a goal—retire and move to Hawaii in ten years. They were frugal, invested every month, but realized that given their present situation, they would be unable to reach their goal.

- How could they retire early? They started by using a spreadsheet to track their monthly income and expenses. *The spreadsheet made them see the obvious. That is, they needed to sell their home and downsize.*

- "The key is getting people to realize where they are versus where they think they are. This is sometimes best illustrated by creating the spreadsheet." Andrea

- They moved quickly, listing and selling the home, and buying a modest condo not far from their old neighborhood in San Diego.

- "Here we are. We now save and invest 67 percent of our monthly income. It is ours to keep, and it feels great!" Andrea

### Comment

- Few of us will be able to save 67 percent of our income each month, but we can learn from them. The first step: articulate your financial goals. Retirement at a certain age? College for the kids? Travel?

- The next step: track monthly income and expenses. What comes in? What goes out? Where can you cut back? What is a necessary expense? What is unnecessary? Where can you trim the fat?

- Next: Develop a monthly financial plan. What can you cut? What do you need to spend each month on necessities? On discretionary items? How much can you save each month? The 25-50-

25 plan can work for you, but your plan may be different. Talk to your CPA or a fee-based financial adviser who can give you objective feedback. Review and monitor your plan on a regular basis to ensure you are on track.

- Andrea and Michael developed a financial plan that works for them. Develop a financial plan that works for you.

# PART 3

## Diversify Investments
## Via Low Cost Index Funds

# 1. INTRODUCTORY COMMENTS

*"It is as normal for people to own stock in companies as it is for them to own homes and cars"*. Margaret Thatcher, British Prime Minister

- As discussed in Parts 1 and 2 of this book, building wealth starts with financial planning and sound money management. Live modestly. Do not buy too much house. Save and invest each month. The 25–50–25 plan works.

- Everyone must master money management, financial planning, and wealth building. The subjects are required; they are not electives.

- Many find investing a big mystery, but investing in low cost index funds is not rocket science. In fact, it is really pretty simple. So, in the pages ahead we discuss what you need to know and do to build wealth by investing in index funds. We hope you enjoy the journey.

- For a definition and further comment about index funds and investing see the Appendices. Check out "Index Funds: Definition & Comments", "Index Funds vs. Exchange Traded Funds (ETFs)", "Index Funds vs. Hedge Funds" and "Recommended Reading".

# 2. COMPARE AND CONTRAST INVESTMENT OPTIONS

*"If your home is your largest investment, you are in financial trouble"*. Robert Kiyosaki, author, *Rich Dad Poor Dad*

- As investors, inflation is one of our worst enemies. See "Time Value of Money" econedlink.org/lessons and "What will $100.00 be worth in 10-20 years?" observationsandnotes.blogspot.com.

- So the question: What investment offers the best opportunity to obtain returns in excess of inflation? What is the best investment *long term*? See http://www.econ.yale.edu/~shiller/data.htm.

- Few ask these questions when they make decisions about investing or spending money. Few compare and contrast asset classes, think about or understand the long-term returns of different investments.

- *Gold* and *real estate*: The long-term returns from gold, precious metals, and real estate over 100 years are about the same as inflation, that is, approximately 3.5 percent per year.

○ Precious metals do not pay dividends and are worth what a buyer is willing to pay for them. Recommended reading: "Gold, Long a Secure Investment, Loses its Luster", Nathaniel Popper, *The New York Times*, April 10. 2013; "Gold's Shine Fades as Metal Tumbles" by Christian Berthlesen, *The Wall Street Journal,* April 12, 2013

○ Houses are boxes of consumer goods and not surprisingly track the consumer price index. That is, housing prices – over the years – generally track inflation. Investment real estate, unlike gold and silver, is *both* a hedge against inflation and an income-producing asset.

● *Bonds*: The *long-term* returns are approximately 5 percent per year. There were years when bonds declined by as much as 20 percent but such a decline is rare. *Bonds are used both for income and as a hedge or anchor against the volatility of stocks.*

● *Cash:* The asset class some think is the safest, that is, cash, is the riskiest long term. One hundred years from today, a $100 bill will still say $100. But as the years pass, the value of the bill will be continually eroded by inflation.

● *Stocks:* Most think that *stocks* are the riskiest asset class. The truth is that stocks, *long term*, have been shown to be the safest investment. Over the last one hundred years the total return for stocks including dividends has been around 10 percent per year. So, $100 investment in stocks one hundred years ago would now be worth $1,378,000. For a discussion of historical returns, see http://observationsandnotes.blogspot.com/2009/03/average-annual-stock-market-return.html.

● *Pew Research Center*: According to a Pew Research Center study released in April 2013 - pewresearch.org – *wealthier households in America tend to hold more of their worth in stocks and bonds.* Real estate contributes most to the value of less wealthy households. Stocks and bonds tend to make up about 65 percent of the wealth of households with $500,000 or more in net worth; homes contribute just 17 percent to their net worth. In contrast, for households with net worth under $500,000, home values contribute about 50% to net worth and financial holdings about 33 percent. The Pew study focused on the period 2009 to 2011. Home prices were depressed during that period, while the S&P stock index rose 34%. Thus, it is not surprising that households emphasizing financial holdings would increase their wealth.

- *Recommendation:* If you want to achieve wealth and financial security, diversify investments. Ensure that financial holdings play a significant role in your portfolio. What is the right balance of stocks, bonds, real estate and other asset classes in your investment plan? The answer depends on your age, financial goals, and tolerance for risk. See our discussion in "Eight Guidelines to Successful Investing – Guideline Six – Control Risk" below.

- *Recommended reading:* "How Much Does the Stock Market Actually Return?" J. D. Roth, Get Rich Slowly.org, getrichslowly.org/blog/2008/12/16/how-much-does-the stock-market-actually-return

# 3. HOUSES VS. THE STOCK MARKET

## A View from the University of Southern California

*"The average single family house has never been a particularly stellar investment".* Robert Bridges, USC

- See "A Home is a Lousy Investment," Robert Bridges, Professor of Finance and Economics, USC, *Wall Street Journal*, 7/11/2011, where he said, "An analysis of home-price and ownership data for the last 30 years in California indicates that the average single family house has never been a particularly stellar investment."

  ○ Between 1980 and 2010, the median-priced home in California rose by an average of 3.6 percent per year, i.e., about the same as inflation.

  ○ In same thirty-year period, U.S. stocks averaged 11.5 percent per year and after inflation about 8.5 percent per year.

○ Bridges: "So a dollar used to purchase a median-price, single-family California home in 1980 would have grown to $5.63 in 2007 and to $2.98 in 2010. The same dollar invested in the Dow Jones Industrial Index would have been worth $14.41 in 2007 and $11.49 in 2010".

○ Bridges: "Here's another way of looking at the situation. If a disciplined investor who might have considered purchasing that median-price house in 1980 had opted instead to invest the 20% down payment of $19,910 and the normal homeownership expenses (above the cost of renting) over the years in the Dow Jones Industrial Index, the value of his portfolio in 2010 would have been $1,800,016. The stocks would have been worth more than the house by $1,503,196. If the analysis is based on 2007, the stock portfolio would have been worth $2,186,120, exceeding the house value by $1,625,850".

## A View from the University of Vienna

*"Why is housing (in the U. S.) such a popular investment?"*

● See "Why Is Housing Such A Popular Investment? A New Psychological Explanation" by Thomas Stephens and Jean-Robert Traynor, Vienna Center for Experimental Economics, University of Vienna, November 23, 2012; http://www.voxeu.org/article/why-housing-such-popular-investment-new-psychological-explanation

● Highlights of the University of Vienna study include the following:

○ "In the U.S., housing remains a popular investment. This popularity is surprising because, over the post-war period, U.S. house prices have been essentially flat in real terms, while over the same period the U.S. stock markets have risen more than fourfold in real terms."

○ "Many view housing as an attractive investment with good potential, despite meager real capital gains over the long run. We find no evidence that property ownership reduces this bias but do find strong evidence that more education and greater cognitive reflection do. These results suggest that better financial education may reduce this bias towards over-investing in housing."

## A View from Yale University

### *"Do not invest in houses". Robert Shiller*

● "Home prices look remarkably stable when corrected for inflation. Over the 100 years ending in 1990 — before the recent housing boom — *real* home prices rose only 0.2 percent a year, on average" Robert Shiller, Sterling Professor of Economics, Yale University

● Shiller: "Here is a harsh truth about homeownership: Over the long haul, it's hard for homes to compete with the stock market in real appreciation". Recommended reading: "Why Home Prices Change (Or Don't)" Robert Shiller, *The New York Times*, April 13, 2013

## Comment

● *The lesson for owner occupants*:

○ Do not depend on your house for retirement.

○ Think twice before putting too much money into a house, "trading up", or buying a dream house.

○ Diversify investments; ensure that stocks play a significant role in your investment portfolio.

● *The lesson for real estate investors*:

○ Diversify investments; do not put all your money into houses.

○ Buy real estate to obtain a return on investment and as a hedge against inflation. Do not expect a house to compete with the stock market in terms of real appreciation.

# 4. INVESTMENT ACCOUNTS

*"Be sensible and store up precious treasures"*.
Proverbs 21.20, Contemporary English Version

- Defined benefit plans or pensions are almost a thing of the past. Increasingly, both private and public sector employers are eliminating defined benefit plans for employees.

- As a result, *you* are now in charge of *your* retirement planning.

- Unfortunately, only a small percentage of people think about the importance of planning for retirement. Of those we counsel, less than 50 percent have an investment account. These include people in the top 10 percent of all income earners. Of those who have investment accounts, few have any significant money invested in them.

- The lesson: If you don't have an investment account, open one today; you do not want to rely on Social Security when you retire. Suggested brokerages to consider:

  ○ Vanguard: vanguard.com – 877-662-7447

    O  T. Rowe Price: troweprice.com – 800-541-6066

    O  Schwab: schwab.com – 866-855-9102

- After you open and fund an investment account, leave the money in the account; let it work for you. Do not make the mistake that many/some make, that is, do not borrow against the account or do not take the money out and spend it. See "Loans Borrowed Against Pensions Squeeze Retirees", Jessica Silver-Greenberg, *New York Times*, April 27, 2013;

- Recommended reading: "Is a Roth IRA Right for You?" by Jane Bryant Quinn, aarp.org/bulletin, April 2013; "Retirement Basics: IRA or 401(k)?" by Scott Holsopple, USNews.com/money, February 4, 2013; "Understanding the ROTH 401(k)" by Alexkandra Todorova, SmartMoney.com, February 5, 2013; and "Save More with a ROTH IRA and 401(k)" by Steve Vernon, Money Watch CBS, CBSNews.com;

# 5. TAX DEFERRED INVESTMENT ACCOUNTS

## a. 401(k) – Employer Sponsored Plans

*"When employees leave their company, many withdraw their 401(k) money and then have no savings or investments".* Dory Laramore, financial writer and certified registered tax preparer

*"Borrowing from or cleaning out your account can come with consequences, the most dire being you won't have enough money to live on during retirement".* Karen Blumenthal, *Wall Street Journal*

- Two types—the traditional and the Roth: In a traditional 401(k), employee contributions are deducted from your taxes. At retirement, withdrawals are taxed at ordinary rates. In a ROTH 401(k), contributions are made with after tax dollars; the withdrawals may be tax free.

- In a 401(k), employers may match employee contributions by as much as fifty cents on the dollar, a huge return. So, contribute as much as possible and get the full employer match. The maximum tax-deferred contributions are set by law. See your employer, tax counsel or review irs.gov.

- 401(k) plans have limitations: Investment decisions are left to you, but investment options are limited. *Expenses can be high— extremely high—or hidden.* Less than half the plans offer a bond index fund. Only one-fourth offer real estate investment funds. Government regulations now require that employers reveal the expense ratios for the plans, showing the cost per $1,000 invested. So, you may be able to compare what your employer offers with what is available on the open market. See Elizabeth O'Brien's comments below.

- Recommended reading: "How Good Is Your Company's 401(k)?", by Kelly Green, *The Wall Street Journal*, January 4, 2013, and *"10 Things 401(k) Plans Won't Tell You – How out of control fees and below par investment options could delay your retirement – or rob you of it entirely,"* by Elizabeth O'Brien, *Smartmoney.com, The Wall Street Journal*, November 12, 2012. Highlights from Ms. O'Brien's article are set forth below:

   ○ "For more and more Americans, the quality of one's retirement comes down to the quality of one's 401(k)."

   ○ 401(k) plans, first introduced in the 1970s, were not originally designed to carry the burden of future retirement. They were intended as "mere supplements" to defined benefit plans or pensions.

   ○ Workers are now on their own when it comes to figuring out how much to save for a comfortable retirement. "Once they stop working, it's up to workers to figure out how to turn a nest egg into an income stream."

○ "The burden on employees to provide for their own financial security is huge, and the best advice companies can give is simply to encourage their workers to save."

○ According to the Employee Benefit Research Institute, the amount by which employee savings and Social Security will fall short of what they need is $4.3 trillion. "Clearly, folks aren't setting aside enough for their post-work lives."

○ "Employers and employees alike often have little idea what they are paying for, thanks to buried 401(k) fees. For example, a fund's expense ratio can encompass everything from marketing fees paid to the investment firm to commissions paid to the broker who recommends particular funds."

○ You may lose years' worth of savings due to 401(k) fees: "A worker who makes $75,000 per year and saves 8% of that annually in a 401(k) would lose 2.8 years' worth of savings in a fund with a 0.2% fee and 11.6 years in one with a 1% fee over the course of a career."

● "Twenty-five percent of assets invested in stocks in a 401(k) are invested in actively managed stock funds and just nine percent are in index funds. Actively managed funds . . . are expensive. Most people will be better off in indexed funds with costs as low as possible." Steve Vernon, Rest-of Life Communications, a benefits consulting firm

● Finally, when you change jobs or retire and move your money from the company's 401(k) to an IRA, be careful about where you move your money. According to the Government Accounting Office, the advice given to employees by money management firms handling company 401(k)s is often misleading and self-serving. "Report finds financial firms' advice on fund rollovers not in the best interest of holders". Washington Post & Associated Press, April 8, 2013.

- So, shop and compare! Go on line; investigate IRA options. Consider Vanguard, T. Rowe Price and Schwab.

## b. Individual Retirement Accounts – IRAs

*"People vastly underestimate how much money it takes to have a lifetime income".* Steve Vernon who helped employers design retirement plans for over 30 years.

- If you do not have access to a company-sponsored 401(k), IRAs are an easy way to invest.

- There are two main types of IRAs—the traditional and the Roth:

  O Contributions to a traditional IRA can be deducted from your taxes, but withdrawals during retirement are taxed at ordinary rates.

  O For the Roth, there are no deductions upfront and may be no taxes when withdrawn during retirement. Which IRA is best for you? Invest in both!

- In IRAs, investment decisions are left to you. The maximum tax deferred contributions are set by law. See your tax counsel for additional information or go to www.irs.gov. IRAs offer virtually unlimited investment options. *You will also be able to shop for the lowest fees possible.* The costs could be less – a great deal less - than a 401(k).

# 6. THE 529 COLLEGE SAVINGS PLAN & THE ROTH

*"Cast your lot with business. Successful investing is about reaping the huge rewards provided by the dividends and earnings of our nation's corporations".* John Bogle, Vanguard founder

- Invest in a college fund for your kids. Tips for parents:

  O Get your child a social security number and open an individual 529 college savings account as soon as possible after birth. Money spent on toys is gone forever. Money invested compounds. Invite relatives to participate.

  O Contributions are made with after tax dollars but taxes on returns are avoided *if* the money is used for qualified educational purposes. See IRS.GOV.

  O Invest in a total U. S. stock market mutual fund or a U. S. small-cap growth index fund, or the equivalent. Avoid conservative investments such as a money market or bond fund during the child's younger years. Note U. S. stocks have averaged approximately 10 percent per year over the long term, while U. S. small-cap stocks have averaged about 12 percent per year long term. $10,000 invested for 18 years at a child's birth into a low cost total U. S. stock market index fund could give you about $55,599 minus the expense ratio charged by the fund. $10,000 invested for 18 years in a small cap fund averaging could give you $76,900 minus the expense ratio. *Historical returns are a guide but do not guarantee future results.*

○ After making an initial investment, invest on a regular basis via auto deduction and stay invested. Do not take the money out until the child is ready for college.

○ Invest frugally. Avoid actively managed funds that charge high fees and expenses, some of which are hidden. Management fees and costs impact significantly on long term returns.

○ Shop and compare what is offered on the market. Consider Vanguard (vanguard.com), T. Rowe Price (troweprice.com) and Schwab (schwab.com).

● Smart Tax Move: Consider a ROTH as another option; consider investing in both a 529 College Plan and a ROTH.

○ Contributions to a ROTH are done with after tax dollars; the money taken out may be tax free.

○ ROTH funds can be withdrawn *without penalty* for educational expenses at any age.

○ In a ROTH the parent can withdraw funds for college expenses for the child or any family member, including the parent.

○ If the child does not go to college, ROTH funds can be used by parents for retirement at age 59½—a win-win situation.

# 7. TAXABLE INVESTMENT ACCOUNTS

*"Investing is the single most effective way to get rich".*
Ramit Sethi, author, *I Will Teach You to Be Rich*

- After contributing to a 401(k) or IRA, the next objective is to investigate, open *and contribute to* taxable investment accounts where contributions are made with after-tax dollars.

  - You can put an unlimited amount of money into taxable investment accounts.

  - Everyone can open a taxable investment account.

  - Investment options are essentially unlimited; see vanguard. com, troweprice.com, and schwab.com.

  - The investment strategy is completely in your hands.

- Most money in taxable investment accounts is invested in actively-managed mutual funds – not the best option.

- *Smart investment move*: *Move to low-cost index funds. Expenses are significantly lower*, and you do not get better results by paying more for actively managed funds. See discussion below.

# 8. INVESTMENT ADVICE AND STRATEGIES

## a. The 2004 Google Teach-ins

*"A winning strategy is to own the nation's publicly held businesses at very low cost. The best way to implement this strategy: Buy an index fund that holds the entire stock market and hold it forever"*. John Bogle, founder of Vanguard who created the index fund in the 1970s

● In 2004, Google, pending a public offering, organized a series of teach-ins to help employees understand investing. Top people in the investment field were invited to speak at Google's offices. The faculty included the following experts:

○ Bill Sharpe, Stanford professor and 1990 Nobel laureate in Economics;

○ Burton Malkiel, Princeton professor and author of *A Random Walk Down Wall Street*;

○ John Bogle, founder of the Vanguard Group and creator of the index fund in the 1970s.

● The faculty made following recommendations:

○ Avoid individual stocks. Avoid actively-managed mutual funds.

○ Diversify and invest in low cost index funds.

○ Invest regularly and automatically.

○ Be careful about spending too much money on financial advisers.

○ Don't try to beat or time the market. Take what the market gives you, and stay invested.

● For a detailed discussion of the 2004 Google Teach-ins, read "The Best Investment Advice You'll Never Get," by Mark Dowie in the January 18, 2008, issue of *San Francisco Magazine*.

## b. A Look at the Best Investment Portfolios in America

*"Most investors are their own worst enemies"*. Ken Fisher, money manager and financial writer, Forbes.com/fisher

● Paul Farrell, "Money Watch," *The Wall Street Journal*, tracked investment portfolios used by Nobel Prize winners, conservative fund managers, and economists. See "Six Reasons Why Wall Street Hates Lazy Portfolios," in the March 27, 2012, issue of the *Wall Street Journal*.

● Farrell learned that these investors do boring, unexciting things with their investments:

○ None buy actively-managed funds or individual stocks sold by brokers or financial planners.

○ They invest regularly and often in low-cost index funds.

○ They buy and hold. They do not trade or try to time the market.

○ They use low-cost Vanguard index funds.

○ They ignore the daily financial news and noise of Wall Street.

# 9. AVOID COMMON MISTAKES

## a. Do Not Trust Your Financial Instincts

*"Don't join the herd. The public buys the most at the top and the least at the bottom"*. Bob Farrell, founder, Farrell's Ice Cream Parlor

- "Our investing intuition is often wrong." Daniel Kahneman, PhD in Psychology, Nobel Prize in Economics, 2002.

  ○ *Our biggest mistake—we buy stocks when prices go up, but when prices fall, we panic and sell.*

  ○ *As a result, the typical investor underperforms the market, getting between zero and three percent per year, not 10 percent per year.*

- Dr. Kahnenam's advice: For most people, a passive approach is wise, that is, buy into low-cost index funds on a regular basis and leave them alone.

- Recommended reading: "Big Money Mistakes You Could Be Making Right Now", Veronica Dagher, *Wall Street Journal*, July 21, 2013

## b. Read History to Become a Better Investor

*"Opportunities abound in America. The gross domestic product on an inflation-adjusted basis has more than quadrupled over the last six decades. Throughout that period, every tomorrow has been uncertain. America's destiny, however, has always been clear: ever-increasing abundance"*. Warren Buffet

- In a recent interview available on line, Mr. Buffett reminded us of the following:

  ○ In the 20th century, the United States endured two World Wars, the Great Depression, twelve recessions, financial panics, and many other challenges.

  ○ Despite the above, over a one-hundred-year period, U.S. stock prices overall averaged about 10 percent per year. On January 1, 1900, the Dow was at 66; on December 31, 1999, at the end of the century, the Dow was at 11,500.

  ○ Bad things happen. The times are always uncertain. Stock prices go up and down, but over time, companies do well and stock prices follow.

- Walter Updegrave, CNNMONEY also put the discussion into historical perspective. He wrote: "Since 1929, we've had 14 recessions and 13 bear (down) markets, an average of about one of each every six or so years. And each time stock prices eventually recovered from these setbacks and climbed to new highs. I see no reason for that dynamic to change." "Market Timing: Not a Good Strategy," *CNN.MONEY.com*, December 13, 2012.

- The lesson: People who invest regularly and stay the course for the long-term achieve substantial wealth.

- Recommended reading: "Market Rewarded Those Who Stuck It Out – A Tale of Three Investors" by Joe Light, *Wall Street Journal,* March 5, 2013 and "Reasons to Avoid Buying Stocks, and Why You Should Ignore Them" by Paul Sullivan, *New York Times*, February 22, 2013.

# 10. EIGHT GUIDELINES TO SUCCESSFUL INVESTING

## a. One: Start Investing Early; Take Advantage of Compounding

*"No one saves a million dollars at once; they save a hundred dollars over and over again".* Stuart Ritter, T. Rowe Price

*"Compounding is mankind's greatest invention. It allows for the huge accumulation of wealth".* Albert Einstein

- "Compounding, also known as compound interest, is the ability of an asset to generate earnings, which are then reinvested in order to generate their own earnings. *In other words, compounding refers to generating earnings from previous earnings."* (Investopedia.com.)

- Start early! Here are a few examples to consider:

  O "No matter how aggressive the portfolio, projected portfolio balances at age 65 are significantly higher for investors who started saving at an early age than for investors who began later in life." Maria Bruno, Vanguard Group

○ "For an individual who invested 6% of their salary in a portfolio of 50% stocks and 50% bonds starting at age 25, the median portfolio balance at retirement was $360,000. The number fell to $237,000 for those who started at age 35 and to $128,000 for those who started at age 45." Carolyn Geer, interviewing Maria Bruno, *The Wall Street Journal*, May 27, 2012

○ If you start at age five, you would need to invest $40 per month and average 10 percent a year to have $1.5 million at age 65. If you start at age forty, however, you would need to invest $2,208 per month and average 10% per year to have $1.5 million at age 65.

● Here is another example of compounding: Recall our friends Marcy and Antoine. Based upon the math, they decided not to buy a $500,000 home, choosing instead to rent and invest both the $100,000 down payment and the $6,000 saved each year on a mortgage. How would they fare if they were to invest the funds into a small-cap index fund that averaged 12.7 percent per year, as opposed to a total U.S. stock market fund that averaged 10.4 percent per year?

● First a little background: Over a period of eighty years, small cap stocks (companies worth less than two billion) beat large-cap stocks by an average of 2.3 percent per year. From 1926 to 2006, the long-term return of the S&P 500 (large companies) was 10.4 percent, while the average annual return of small-cap stocks during the same period was 12.7 percent. Robert Brokamp, "Beginning Investing Strategies: Small-Cap Investing," TheMotleyFool.com

- So, if Marcy and Antoine were to invest in a small-cap index fund earning an average annual return of 12.7 percent per year, their $100,000 in principal could potentially grow to $3,612,000 in 30 years minus the fund's expense ratio. Their $6,000 invested every year for 30 years could grow to $2,086,503.50 minus the expense ratio. Not bad! *Historical returns are a guide but do not guarantee future results.*

- *Important caveat:* Compound interest can be your friend and work for you. Or, it can be your enemy and work against you. Do you have a high-interest credit card and make the minimum payment each month? Compound interest is now working for the credit card company not you.

- *Takeaway:* (1) Start to invest today. Allow compounding to work for you. (2) Get rid of debt, especially high-interest credit card debt; do not let compounding work against you.

- *Recommended reading:* "So You Think You're A Financial Genius?" by Carolyn T. Geer, Wall Street Journal, June 23, 2013. Ms. Geer points out that many investors – one quarter in an education foundation survey –do not understand compound interest. Nor do many investors understand how Wall Street's take cuts into earnings. "Investors end up paying all manner of fees . . . . The longer the investment period, the bigger Wall Street's take". See Part "Invest Frugally" below.

- If you would like more information on compound interest, read "Albert Einstein's Greatest Discovery: "The Rule of 72" by L. E. Duncan, http://voices.yahoo.com/albert-einsteins-greatest-discovery-rule-72, December 12, 2006; also see "Ten Facts about Compound Interest," by Gary Foreman, *U.S. News & World Report*, November 19, 2012, http://money.msn.com/personal-finance/10-facts-about-compound-interest.

## b. Two: Invest Regularly and Stay Invested

*"Our favorite holding period is forever"*. Warren Buffett

*"Bad news is an investor's dream; it lets you buy stocks at a marked-down price. Stocks always come out of crisis"*. Warren Buffet

- Systematic investing and dollar cost averaging are two approaches to maximize saving and investing. Systematic investing is setting up an automatic deposit from your checking account into an investment account on a regular basis. The reduction to your pay will not be noticed, and you will not be influenced by negative market news. Dollar cost average is a similar concept and means you buy into the market over a period at different price levels.

- It is important that you invest regularly and that you stay invested. Reinvest the dividends; take advantage of compounding. You will build a nest egg over many years.

- "The two levers an investor can control—*savings time horizon and savings rate*—will provide a higher probability of success rather than relying on the possibility for higher portfolio returns with more aggressive investments." Maria Bruno, Vanguard

## c. Three: Diversify Investments

*"98 or 99 percent—maybe more than 99 percent - of the people who invest should extensively diversify and not trade. That leads them to an index fund with very low costs"*. Warren Buffet

## Core Funds to Consider

- Vanguard Total U.S. Stock Market Index Fund: This fund gives an investor ownership in the shares of virtually every publically-traded stock in the United States. The Vanguard expense ratio for a $1,000 investment each year (ER) is .05/yr.

- Vanguard Total U.S. Bond Market Index Fund: This fund gives an investor ownership in the shares of the entire taxable United States investment grade bond market, including government and corporate issues. Vanguard expense ratio is .11/yr.

## Consider Global Investments

- Profound changes are occurring in the global economy.

  O *Foreign markets* led by China, India, and Brazil account for more than one-half of the world's economy.

  O *Emerging markets* are growing three times faster than the United States, Japan, and European nations.

- The United States is seldom among the top ten stock markets in the world. The top country changes every year. So, diversify by investing in foreign markets. Consider investing in a total international fund.

- The lesson: Ignoring foreign markets may mean missing investment opportunities.

## A Global Core Fund to Consider

- Vanguard's Total International Stock Market Index Fund:

○ This fund offers investors a low-cost way to gain equity exposure to both developed and emerging international economies. The fund tracks stock markets all over the globe, with the exception of the United States.

○ Because it invests in non-U.S. stocks, including both developed and emerging markets, the fund can be more volatile than a domestic fund.

○ Long-term investors who want to add a diversified international equity position to their portfolio might want to consider this fund as an option. The expense ratio is 0.18 percent/yr.

## Consider Real Estate Investment Trusts

*"REITS deserve a small percentage in your portfolio."*
David Swenson, Fund Manager, Yale University

*"Real Estate Investment Trusts (REITS) are mutual funds that buy stocks in companies that own real estate-related assets such as office buildings, shopping malls, apartments, storage facilities, and hotels."* Roger J. Brown, Ph.D., past Director of Research for the Real Estate & Land Use Institute, San Diego State University

● Some REITs invest nationally, some are confined to a local geographic area and some invest throughout the world.

● REITs pass nearly all their income as dividends to shareholders, but the dividends are taxed as ordinary income—not the long term capital gains dividends of stocks.

● Advantage of REITs: They are not in lock step with the stock market. Bonds prices will fall if inflation and interest rates rise in an improving economy. REITS could thrive.

- Disadvantage of REITS: They are stocks and thus subject to the ups and downs of the market. They are more "risky" than bonds but may deserve some percentage in your portfolio.

- Recommended reading: "The Best Place to Hold REIT's: An IRA or Taxable Account?" Gregory Zuckerman, June 7, 2013, *Wall Street Journal*

## d. Four: Invest Frugally

*"Index funds have far outperformed the active manager and at a far lower cost to the investor"*. Burton Malkiel, Princeton University*

- Investment costs have a substantial impact on a portfolio's performance. "Whether you'll have enough money for retirement depends on more than how much you save and which investments you pick. The other powerful factor is how much you pay for those investments. . . . There is no evidence that paying more gets you better returns—quite the opposite. Small investors are far better off keeping costs to a minimum with low-cost investment options such as index funds." Liz Weston, MSN.com

- The U.S. Labor Department: "Assume that you are an employee with thirty-five years until retirement and a current 401(k) account balance of $25,000. If returns on investments in your account over the next 35 years average 7% and fees and expenses reduce your average returns by 0.5%, your account balance will grow to $227,000 at retirement, even if there are no further contributions to your account. If fees and expenses are 1.5% your account balance will grow to only $163,000. The 1% difference in fees and expenses would reduce your account balance at retirement by 28%."

- Maria Bruno, Vanguard Group: "Take an investor, age 25, who contributes annually to a portfolio that is 50% stocks and 50% bonds. If the investor selects an actively managed fund with an expense ratio of 1.25% versus a low-cost index fund with an expense ratio of 0.25%, the difference in the median ending balance at retirement would be nearly $100,000.00 ($540,000 versus $456,000) or a loss of roughly 20% in the portfolio's value."

- Also consider taxes and brokerage fees: The typical actively managed fund trades all stocks in the fund each year, triggering short-term capital gains and brokerage fees paid by investors who own the shares. In addition to high expense ratios, actively-managed funds can charge investors fees for sales and marketing costs. Some actively-managed funds charge sales commissions of 6 percent, either up front or at the time the investor sells their shares.

- So, bottom line: You do not get what you pay for. Long-term, actively-managed funds do not give investors better returns than low-cost index funds that track he market.

- *Recommended reading: "You're Paying too Much for Investment Help", Burton Malkiel, *Wall Street Journal*, May 28, 2013

### e. Five: Do Not Try To Time the Market

*"Ignore the guy who tells you he can beat the market".*
Carl Richards, Certified Financial Planner, author
and contributor to *The New York Times*

- As an investor, you will undoubtedly be solicited by "advisers" in the financial services industry who will tell you they sell actively managed funds that perform better than the overall market. If you contact a large, brokerage company they may give you the same sales pitch. Ignore them! Some actively-managed funds do "beat the market" for a short period but not the long-term. So, if you are ever tempted to buy one of these funds, read Carl Richard's article, "A Warning about That Guy Who Is Beating the Market," in the December 11, 2012, issue of *The New York Times*.

- The truth is that stock markets are irrational. No one can know the best days before they occur. *Its time in the market that matters.* As Ramit Sethi says, in *I Will Teach You to be Rich*, "No one can time the market." From 1983 to 2003, the S&P index averaged 10 percent per year. During this twenty-year period, if you missed the best twenty days, your return fell to 5.03 percent per year. If you missed the best fifty days, your return fell to 1.6 percent per year.

## f. Six: Control Risk

*"Your investment plan should include an allocation among stocks, bonds and other assets".* Andrea Coombes, *Wall Street Journal*

*"Asset allocation is the most important investment decision you will make".* Brendan Erne, *"Seven Deadly Investor Sins," Forbes*

- Risk can be controlled in a portfolio by asset allocation. Do not put all your money into stocks. Do not put all your money into bonds. Hold stocks for growth and income. Hold bonds as a hedge or defense against the short-term volatility of stocks. Thus, bonds play an important role in portfolio diversification.

- For example, if you were to invest $100,000 in a 100 percent stock portfolio and stock prices fell by 20 percent, you would have a significant loss. On the other hand, if you invest $100,000 in a 50/50 stock/bond portfolio and stock prices fell by 20 percent, the bonds would serve as a buffer. In fact, the bonds in your portfolio would probably go up in value, offsetting some of the losses with stocks. In addition, you are now in a position to take some of the money invested in bonds and buy stocks at a lower price.

- But note the counsel of Maria Bruno at Vanguard: "The amount one ended up with at retirement was influenced more by how much one saved than by how the money was invested. Saving 9 percent of ones salary in a 50/50 stock bond portfolio, starting at age 25, resulted in a higher median ending balance—about $540,000—than saving 6 percent at age 25 in a more aggressive account of 80 percent stock and 20 percent bonds—about $470,000."

## What is the Right Balance of Stocks and Bonds?

*"Bonds are your portfolio's shock absorbers"*. Allan S. Roth, author "How a Second Grader Beats Wall Street," and financial writer for CBS Moneywatch.com

*"You should own more stocks than bonds"*. Bill Gross, financial manager who runs PIMCO's $270.0 billion Total Return Fund.

*"Bonds are a terrible investment at the moment (May 2013). Owners of long- term bonds may see big losses when interest rates eventually rise"*. Warren Buffet

- Investor *guideline*: The percentage of stocks in your portfolio could equal 120 minus your age. If you want to be more conservative, your percentage could be 100 minus your age. The right balance of stocks and bonds in your portfolio, however, depends on your financial goals and tolerance for risk.

- For example, Warren Buffet, in his eighties, is reportedly 100 percent invested in stocks. Few, if any, eighty-year-olds, however, will want to follow Mr. Buffett's lead. The short-term returns in stocks can be disappointing. In 2008, when the market fell, many investors were caught with substantially all their money in stocks. So, at least five years before retirement, you may want to start to move your money to more conservative investments.

- John Bogle, founder of Vanguard, also in his eighties, is reportedly 80 percent invested in bonds and 20 percent in stocks.

- Mark Laturno, age nineteen, Gary's son, is 90 percent invested in stocks and 10 percent in bonds.

- A typical corporate pension fund is invested 60 percent in stocks and 40 percent in bonds. Vanguard's Balanced Index Fund matches this 60/40 split, stocks vs. bonds, by tracking two indexes that represent broad barometers for the U.S. equity and U.S. taxable bond markets. Expense ratio on for this fund is 0.10 percent/yr.

- Life cycle or target date funds are another option. They match the stock/bond mix with your age. Both TR Price and Vanguard offer target date funds. They may work for hands-off investors because they periodically rebalance without the investor owner taking any action. Recommended: "Missing the Target", Liam Pleven & Joe Light, June 14, 2013, *Wall Street Journal*.

- *Recommended reading*: "Social Security's Role in Your Retirement Portfolio" by Walter Updegrave, CNN Money, February 20, 2013;

- "When Interest Rates Rise, Watch Out" by Andy Kessler, *The Wall Street Journal,* February 21, 2013; "Low Interest Rates Force Creative Choices" by Anand Shefali, *The Wall Street Journal,* March 1, 2013; "What Are CDs Good For?" by Liam Pleven, *Wall Street Journal*, March 15, 2013; "The Dark Side of Bonds" in the Appendices.

- *A note about interest rates*: Interest rates today (2013) are at historically low levels. When interest rates go up, bond prices, especially long term bond funds, will fall. Warren Buffet has been quoted as saying that he does not like owning bonds "right now", and he does not think average investors should either. His recommendation for individual investors (as of May 2013) is to keep cash on hand if the unexpected happens. See "Warren Buffett: Buy Stocks; Beware Bonds" USA Today, May 6, 2013.

- Depending on interest rates, as an alternative to Vanguard's Total U.S. Bond Market Index Fund which invests in all maturities – short, intermediate and long term bonds - one might consider a short term bond fund that would be less vulnerable to interest rate risk. Vanguard's Short Term Bond Fund offers maturities from one to five years. Another option would be to use a money market fund in lieu of a bond fund. Vanguard's Prime Money Market Fund *seeks* to provide current income and preserve a shareholders' principal investment by maintaining a share price of $1.00. The fund invests in short-term, high-quality securities. The amount of income that a shareholder may receive will be largely dependent on the prevailing interest-rate environment.

- Recommended reading: "Hidden Danger Lurks in Long-Term Bond Funds" John Waggoner, USA Today, April 26, 2013; "Making Sense of Money Market Funds", vanguard.com; "Why Your Portfolio Still Needs Bonds", Carolyn T. Geer, Wall Street Journal, July 21, 2013.

- But shop and compare. Suggested brokerages to contact:

  O  Vanguard: vanguard.com – 877-662-7447

  O  T. Rowe Price: troweprice.com – 800-541-6066

  O  Schwab: schwab.com – 866-855-9102

## Keep Your Portfolio Tuned Up

- If you let your portfolio roam free for too long, you could become too heavily invested in stocks, risking large losses if the market were to go down.

- How do you rebalance? Buy or sell securities to get back to your preferred asset mix. Vanguard will rebalance automatically for you if you give them the authority to do so.

- Recommended reading: "Asset Allocation and Disciplined Rebalancing" Vanguard.com, April 15, 2013; "Keeping Your Investments in Balance", Carolyn T. Geer, *Wall Street Journal*, June 8, 2013.

## For Some, Asset Mix May Not Be Significant

*Center for Retirement Research, Boston College Study*

- According to the Boston College study, few in United States have enough money invested in their accounts to make a difference.

Improved investment returns by asset allocation and rebalancing for these people may not significant.

- The following variables would be more important for most people: (1) continue to work: for every year worked, it is a year you can add to your retirement portfolio and not take money from it; and (2) cut spending and increase savings.

## g. Seven: Keep Your Portfolio Simple

*"When it comes to your portfolio and investing practice, more isn't always better".* Anna Prior, *Wall Street Journal*

- When it comes to investments, we have many options. "Some investors think they are diversified because they have money in 10 different places, only to find there's a lot of overlap". Scott Halliwell, certified financial planner, USAA.

- Sometimes we are overwhelmed by the options available to us. One person who called me to consult said, "My financial planner has me in over a dozen actively managed mutual funds. I am overwhelmed so I let him manage my portfolio and decide what to buy and sell". Not smart! Recommendations and guidelines:

  O First: Do not use the same financial adviser to counsel you on a financial plan and also buy investment products. Such an adviser has a conflict of interest. You are now a part of his/her financial plan.

  O Second: Switch to low cost index funds.

  O Three: You only need a few funds. For example, if you are in your teens, twenties or even thirties you may be comfortable with one fund: a total U. S. stock market index fund or a small- cap growth index fund. If you are more conservative, you may want to add a total bond market index fund or a money market fund for income and as a hedge against the volatility of stocks. As the years go on, most investors add a bond fund to their portfolio. To add diversity, some/many will add a total international stock index fund and possibly a REIT index fund. In some cases a single fund can take the place of several funds. The classic example is a target-date fund discussed earlier in this section. The fund company automatically adjusts your mix of stocks and bonds to get more conservative as you near retirement.

○ Four: Put investing on auto pilot via monthly auto deductions from your bank and then monitor your portfolio; rebalance on an annual basis if necessary.

● Recommended reading: "Keep Your Portfolio Simple" Anna Prior, *Wall Street Journal*, May 2, 2013.

## f. Eight: Stay Married

*"The most important decision you make in life
is who you marry".* Warren Buffet

If you are married, stay married. *The average married couple saves ten times more than the average single person.* Why the huge disparity? The answer: divorce. Couples who divorce typically spend a great deal on attorneys and must also obtain new housing. It is cheaper for two to live than one. See the April 21, 2013, Wall Street Journal video on personal finance, captioned "Stay Married and You'll Retire with More Savings". Also see "Couples Need More Than Love" in the Appendices.

# 11. FINANCIAL PLANNERS AND OTHER ADVISERS

## a. Do You Need a Financial Adviser?

*"Many people need a financial planner"*. Larry Branton, Esq., tax, estate planning and employee benefits attorney

- Jane Bryant Quinn, author, "Making the Most of Your Money," gives this advice:

  O Financial planning is not that hard. You do not need a financial planner.

  O You do need a list of objectives, a few simple financial products (such as index funds), a timeframe to give investments time, reasonable expectations, and the ability to avoid sales pitches—that is, avoid pitches from individuals in the financial services industry who sell actively-managed mutual funds and individual stocks.

- Ms. Quinn gives sound advice. We have seen first- hand, however, that it is difficult for people to make wise judgments about their financial situations. So, we believe that "many" people, as Mr. Branton states, could benefit from a financial adviser.

- *But be careful:* Hire a planner or adviser to review and/or assist with your financial plan. Do not allow the planner to sell investment products to you.

- *Recommendation:* Buy low cost index funds directly from a large discount broker such as Vanguard, Schwab, or T. Rowe Price. See our discussion immediately below.

## b. Is Your Adviser a Fiduciary or a Salesperson?

*"The people most in need of honest financial advice . . . don't realize that their so- called adviser isn't an adviser at all, but a salesman".* Tara Bernard Siegel, New York Times, July 26, 2013

*"There is no federal requirement for financial brokers who give advice and earn commissions to act in the best interest of their clients".* "Investors Beware", *New York Times,* February 15, 2013

- A RAND Corporation study revealed that investors have little understanding of whether their financial planner is a fiduciary or salesperson or how their planner is paid, that is, commission based, an hourly rate, or a percentage of the client's portfolio.

- Allan Roth, CPA and Financial Planner, "The Two Faces of Your Financial Planner," *AARP Magazine*, April/May 2012, offers the following advice:

  O Do not use planners to buy investment products.

  O Planners who sell investment products are not fiduciaries; they in fact have a conflict of interest with clients.

- Andrew Haigney, a registered investment advisor, offers these insights:

  O "Investment advisers and planners effectively have a license to steal.

  O "One needs to understand that the financial services industry's planning-based sales techniques were developed by the marketing folks on Wall Street. Years ago traditional stockbrokers struggled to get a handle on the true nature of their client's assets. Very often their most wealthy clients would maintain small accounts with the brokers.

  O "By offering their customers planning-based products and services, the customers became more forthright about revealing the true nature of their assets. The more details clients reveal about their financial station, the more sales opportunities for the financial services firms.

  O "When your financial plan comes with a financial planner or an investment adviser, you actually handicap your chances of achieving your goals. Investors seeking help putting together a financial plan end up becoming a part of the financial planner's financial plan".

- Haigney's article, "Your Financial Planner Will Probably Handicap Every Investment You Make," can be read at http://www.businessinsider.com/a-license-to-steal-2012-8#ixzz25RfXccF3.

- Other recommended articles: "A Start -Up Aims to Bring Financial Planning Advice to the Masses", *New York Times*, July 26, 2013, and "A Fancy Financial Adviser Does Not Ensure High Standards", *New York Times,* July 6, 2012.

# c. Recommendations

- Retain a tax adviser to review your investment plan. S/he can ensure that your money is invested in the "correct" accounts, that is, taxable or tax deferred. The goal is to decrease taxes and increase savings. See Chapter 12 immediately below.

- Retain estate-planning counsel to create a living trust to ensure that your assets pass directly to your beneficiaries, thus avoiding probate. Equally important, a living trust will allow your heirs to manage your estate in the event you become incapacitated.

- Retain a trusted fiduciary to review your financial plan. A fiduciary can evaluate your plan and give you an opinion as to whether your plan is reasonable and wise. Your adviser could be a CPA, an economist, an MBA in Finance, or a financial planner. The rules of engagement should include the following:

  - Understand how this adviser will be paid. Ensure s/he is a fiduciary who represents your interests.

  - Do not allow this person to sell you financial products such as actively-managed mutual funds, stocks or annuities.

  - Ensure that the person you select understands money management, financial planning, and wealth building.

  - If you need help constructing your portfolio or managing your investments, a fee-only planner who charges by the hour may be located at garrettplanningnetwork.com.

  - Recommended reading: "How to Find Low Cost Investment Help," by Michael Pollock, *Wall Street Journal*, May 31, 2012; "A New Era for Do-It-Yourself Investing", WSJ, May 6, 2013

# 12. TAX EFFICIENT INVESTING

*"Improper tax management can cost you more than 25 percent of your long- term return, severely impacting your spending power in retirement"*. Brendan Erne, financial writer

- "The two most common tax missteps are failing to use a 401(k) or IRA and using tax inefficient investment vehicles such as actively managed mutual funds." Brendan Erne

- "While it is probably a poor idea to own actively-managed mutual funds, it is a terrible idea to own them in taxable accounts. Taxes are a drag on performance of up to four percentage points each year. Many low cost index funds allow your capital gains to grow largely undisturbed until you sell." William Bernstein, author of *The Four Pillars of Investing*

  O Note the managers of actively-managed funds, attempting to beat the overall market, typically sell or turn over the stocks in their funds on a regular basis, thus triggering short-term capital gains. Taxes paid by investors, as stated by Dr. Bernstein, are a significant drag on the fund's performance.

○ "Index funds are tax friendly, allowing investors to defer capital gains or avoid them completely if the shares are later bequeathed (that is, left to heirs). Taxes are an important financial consideration because the earlier realization of capital gains will substantially reduce net returns." Dr. Burton Malkiel, author of *A Random Walk Down Wall Street* and Princeton professor

● Recommended reading: "How to Be Smarter About Taxes" By Michael A. Pollock, *The Wall Street Journal*, February 2, 2013

# 13. WILL YOUR MONEY LAST YOUR LIFETIME?

*"For many retirees, the big risk isn't that they will run out of money before they turn 70 but after 85".* Brett Arends, *Wall Street Journal*

- Many of us now live into our eighties, nineties, and even to one hundred. Perhaps the biggest challenge will be to ensure that our savings will last our lifetime. How can we ensure that it does? First, be careful before moving to all cash, certificates of deposit, or bonds, which may not keep up with inflation. You must invest some of your portfolio in stocks.

- How then should you allocate among stocks, bonds, CDs, cash or money market funds? How much can you withdraw each year and ensure your money will last as long as you need it?

  ○ "In the 1990's California financial planner William Bengen analyzed historical returns of stocks and bonds and found that portfolios with 60% of their holdings in large company stocks and 40% in intermediate term U. S. bonds could sustain withdrawal rates starting at 4.15% and adjusted each year for inflation for every 30 -year span going back to 1926 - 1955". Kelly Greene, *Wall Street Journal. Can you rely on the 4% rule today?* See citation to Ms. Greene's article below.

○ "If you want reasonable assurance your savings will support you at least 30 years, the single most important thing you can do is to start with a modest withdrawal rate – say 4% or, given today's interest rates, perhaps even less". Walter Updegrave, CNN Money

○ "To avoid running out of money too soon – or ending up with a big stash late in retirement, along with regrets you hadn't spent more freely early on – you've got to remain flexible, cutting back when returns are lean and perhaps spending more if your portfolio's done especially well." See "Make Your Retirement Savings Last into Your 90's" by Walter Updegrave, CNN Money, March 15, 2013.

● *Recommended*: Pick up a financial calculator. MSN.com, Bloomberg.com and bankrate.com, among others, have on line calculators if you do not own one. Put in the amount you have saved to date and then run a number of scenarios with different withdrawal rates and different stock/bond allocations to get an idea of how long your money will last. If you are uncomfortable using a calculator, you may want to consult a financial adviser or a friend who is comfortable using one. See Chapter 11 where we discuss how to locate and select a competent adviser to assist you.

● *Recommended reading*: See "Say Goodbye to the 4% Rule" by Kelly Green, *Wall Street Journal,* March 1, 2013. Ms. Green suggests three alternative approaches that retirement specialists opine may work better than the 4% rule: 1.) Use annuities in your portfolio instead of bonds; 2.) Follow the minimum IRS rules for IRA withdrawals; 3.) Peg withdrawals to stock valuations.

- One final question: Is it possible to be a conservative investor and not outlive your money? The challenge: you must be an aggressive saver. "Save half of what you make; live on the other half," Mark Twain.

- Good news: conservative investors who save aggressively can do OK. Gary's dad invested in government bonds and a four unit apartment building, and his nest egg that lasted years beyond his lifetime. It is now being used to take care of our step mother who is well into her 90's.

- Today, consider the following facts:

  ○ Government I Bonds pay a fixed interest rate, (0 currently) and a variable rate that keeps pace with inflation.

  ○ TIPS–Treasury Inflation-Protected Securities pay a fixed interest rate plus their principal is adjusted by the Consumer Price Index.

  ○ The returns on TIPS and I Bonds are about the same as inflation.

- Recommended reading: "The Experts: Finding Income Despite Low Interest Rates", *Wall Street Journal*, March 6, 2013

# PART 4

## Investing in Houses

## Pros & Cons, Biggest Mistakes, and Guidelines for Investors

# 1. INTRODUCTORY COMMENTS

*"Investing in a rental home isn't as safe as it may seem"*.
Tara Siegel Bernard, *New York Times,* March 30, 2013

*"Buying real estate is the largest, most complicated and riskiest purchase you will ever make"*. Leonard Baron, investor and author

- Investing in real estate is elective not mandatory. Warren Buffet, America's most successful investor, for example, does just fine buying companies. Because many people want to be real estate investors we have included this section. The opinions we express are based on our experiences buying, owning and managing single family houses for the last thirty years, as well as counseling real estate investors for the last ten years. The opinions expressed are also based on my experiences as an attorney, mediator, and arbitrator resolving real estate disputes.

- Both real estate and stock market investing require knowledge, commitment, and patience. Investing in low cost index funds is not complicated. In fact, as we have seen, it is pretty simple. If you invest by auto deduction month after month, year after year, you can build a nest egg, take advantage of compounding, and achieve wealth and financial security.

- Real estate investing, on the other hand, is not as simple or safe as it may appear. We have seen many people try to be real estate investors. We have seen many fail.

- If you want to be a real estate investor, learn as much as you can *before* you get started. In addition to reading this part of our book, read Part 3, in particular Chapters 2 and 3, "Compare and Contrast Asset Classes" and "Houses Versus the Stock Market."

- Some of our favorite real estate investment books are listed in the Appendices. See Amazon.com for further information about each book. A few comments about the books and their authors:

- William Nickerson's *How I Turned $1,000 into a Million in Real Estate in My Spare Time* - based on real estate investments in the 1930s – may have been the first manual for the private real estate investor. The book is a classic; many investors today still practice his teachings.

- Roger J. Brown, PhD, a former professor at the University of California, Irvine, and San Diego State University, is the author of *Private Real Estate Investing – Part I, The Basics.* Dr. Brown updates Nickerson's timeless message and elaborates on it in a framework that describes how individual real estate investors make decisions today. The book is aimed at college and graduate level students. A reader will be rewarded with insights unavailable in the typical real estate investment book available to the general public. For the more advanced student/investor, see Dr. Brown's *Private Real Estate Investing, Part II, Risk Analysis and Part III, Special Topics*, as well as his web site – mathestate. com.

● We also recommend books by Leonard Baron, MBA and CPA – ProfessorBaron.com - and John W. Schaub – JohnSchaub.com. Mr. Baron is a San Diego State University lecturer, real estate investor, and author of a number of real estate investment books. Vikki and I have authored several chapters in "Due Diligence 101" identified in the Appendices. Leonard loves to teach, and his students appreciate his counsel and guidance. I occasionally teach classes with him. John Schaub, who resides in Sarasota, Florida, has been teaching seminars to investors for many years. He occasionally offers classes on the West Coast. Check his web site for dates and locations.

● Finally, are you sure you want to be a real estate investor? See the comments by Yale economics professor Robert Shiller, "A Negative View of Real Estate Investing" immediately below. But also see "A Positive View of Real Estate Investing" follow-ing his comments.

● *Recommended reading*: "Investing in a Rental Home Isn't as Safe as It May Seem", Tara Siegel Bernard, *The New York Times*, March 30, 2013; "Why Home Prices Change (Or Don't)" Robert Shiller, *The New York Times*, April 13, 2013; also see "Houses versus the Stock Market" in Part 3 above.

# 2. A NEGATIVE VIEW OF REAL ESTATE INVESTING

*"Housing is a speculative, risky investment"*. Robert Shiller, Yale Professor, economist, and historian of financial data

*"A house can be a good investment, yet only a few actually make money investing in houses"*, John W. Schaub, author, "Building Wealth One House at a Time"

Yale University Professor Robert Shiller was interviewed by Bloomberg News on Wednesday, February 6, 2013. His comments are available at Bloomberg.com/video/shiller.

- From 1890 to 1990, the appreciation in housing factoring out inflation was essentially zero, and housing was not viewed as a great investment. Over the long haul, it's hard for homes to compete with the stock market in real appreciation.

- So, why is housing considered a good investment today? The answer: Investing in housing was a fad idea that took hold around 2000.

- Houses must be maintained; they depreciate and go out of style. All of these are problems. And there is technical progress in housing. The new ones are better.

- People who own houses lose the opportunity to invest their money elsewhere. We are too optimistic about houses. Buy them for their utility and for personal reasons not as an investment vehicle.

# 3. A POSITIVE VIEW OF REAL ESTATE INVESTING

*"Buying one house at a time can make you wealthy"*. John W. Schaub, author, "Building Wealth One House at a Time"

*If you're thinking about retirement, the (rental) income can serve as an inflation-adjusted annuity of sorts, since rents are likely to rise over time"*. Tara Siegel Bernard, *New York Times*

- Despite the negative views above, we have seen ordinary people succeed and build wealth with real estate. All had a plan; none attempted to get rich quick. All used their rental income to pay the mortgage and other costs with the goal of obtaining free and clear houses. Examples of people who succeeded are below.

- A realtor in San Diego, a single woman in her mid- 60's, worked hard all of her life, using the income from real estate transactions to buy single family houses. She then used the rental income to pay the mortgages and now owns four San Diego homes free and clear. The rents from these four properties bring in approximately

$2,000 per house each month. She has four other homes with mortgages; her goal is to own all eight homes free and clear within a few years.

- *Compare and contrast*: Many people in this lady's age group have no retirement savings and are dependent on social security. The average monthly social security check in America – around $1,200 - is less than the income from one of her rentals.

- Gary's parents bought a four-unit building in St. Paul, Minnesota. Rental payments were used to pay the mortgage. His family lived rent free, and his dad diversified his investments by purchasing bonds each month. His parents retired at a young age to a golf course community in Arizona and lived well for many years.

- A realtor in our company observed her dad purchase houses when she was a kid. He used the rent to pay the mortgages. She followed his example and now owns a twelve-unit building in San Diego, as well as numerous single-family and four-unit homes, both in San Diego and Texas.

- The realtor's son followed his mother's example. The family had saved $48,000 for his college but he opted to attend community college. The son used the $48,000 to buy a $95,000 condo in San Diego:

  - He put 50 percent down. The mortgage, HOA, and taxes are $500 per month. The rent is $1,200 per month. Cash flow is $700 per month—a substantial return on investment.

  - His plan is to use 100 percent of the positive cash flow to pay off the condo early.

# 4. BIGGEST MISTAKES BY INVESTORS

*"The first defense is diversification".* John Longo, investment strategist, MDE Group, Morristown, New Jersey

*"You need to have a sizable reserve fund set aside to pay for expenses, whether it's to cover the mortgage when the property is sitting vacant or to make repairs, which novice landlords tend to underestimate".* Kenneth J. Eaton, financial planner, Overland Park, Kansas

Many who attempt to invest in real estate fail. Some of the most common errors we see are:

- Attempting to be an investor without adequate education or training. We have met countless people buying investment homes who had no idea how to carry out due diligence when buying, how to evaluate return on investment, how to be a landlord, or even how to run a credit report.

- Buying with negative cash flow and counting on appreciation. Eventually, these properties are typically lost to foreclosure or sold as short sales. See Part 1, Chapter 6, "Lessons Learned:

Biggest Mistakes – Houses" for examples of people who put significant money into negative cash flow homes for many years.

- Underestimating the cost of maintaining the properties. New investors often underestimate the costs and challenges of owning, maintaining, and managing houses. Houses are a great deal of work. Tenants can be challenging; expenses can be high. Some people love owning houses; many find that it does not work for them.

- Not diversifying investments. "If you have a $600,000 portfolio, putting $300,000 into one asset class is a highly concentrated bet". Sara Siegel Bernard, *New York Times*.

- Not comparing, contrasting or understanding other investment options. Many blindly move forward with real estate investments without first understanding the opportunity to invest in an asset class with the potential for significantly better long term returns. See Part 3, "Compare and Contrast Different Investment Options" and "Houses vs. the Stock Market".

- Buying and owning properties in other states and cities. "I owned houses in 49 states and lost money in 48," Jack Miller, real estate investor, financial mentor and teacher. His point: Your chances of success are best in your community where you can personally take care of the property.

- Overleveraging, financing for the short term, and flipping houses. If you are going to flip houses, see our discussion about the importance of having a plan B in Part 2, Chapter 5 "Financial Plans That Fail."

- Using the property as a piggy bank. Do not take money out of the property beyond the amount originally borrowed. You increase the chance of losing the house to foreclosure. You may also be creating additional tax liability if there is cancellation of debt income in a short sale or foreclosure. *Consult a tax attorney or CPA.*

# 5. GUIDELINES FOR INVESTORS, PART I

*"There is a lot of . . . risk associated with rental income . . . . a lot of things can go wrong".* Christopher J. Mayer, professor of real estate, finance and economics, Columbia Business School

*"Owners who did not take on a lot of debt have been able to hang on".* Paul Sullivan, *New York Times, March 15, 2013*

- Avoid partners. The best partner is no partner. Relationships may start with the best of intentions but turn sour. If you must have a partner, ensure your partnership agreement provides for the mediation of disputes. Avoid costly protracted litigation.

- Avoid fixers, war zones, and high-vacancy areas. Buy single-family houses in nice areas near your home. Entry-level homes are more likely to cash flow. Avoid luxury homes or homes near the beach. They do not cash flow.

- Attempt to buy a property with tenants in place. You get the security deposit and pro-rated rent. You may avoid having to clean, paint, update, or fix too many things in the unit. Ensure that you review the current tenant's lease, credit application, and credit report.

- Buy with cash or get the smallest loan possible. Get a thirty-year amortized loan with a fixed interest rate. Know what your mortgage costs will be in the future. (*Beware:* When you pay all cash or make a large down payment, you lose the opportunity to invest the cash into another investment that may give you a better long term return. Do you want to lose that opportunity? See Part 3, Chapter 2, "Compare and Contrast Investment Options".)

- Ensure the property gives you substantial positive cash flow:

  ○ Ensure the rent covers the mortgage, taxes, maintenance, insurance, vacancy factor (tenants do not stay forever and may default on the rent), monthly HOA, and HOA assessments.

  ○ Use the *price rent ratios* as a guide. See Appendices L.

  ○ Ensure the *return on investment* (ROI) is acceptable to you. Most investors are comfortable with 4 to 6 percent return per year.

    ○ Learn to calculate return on investment. Purchase price, loan terms, appreciation rate, taxes, expenses and other factors must be considered when you evaluate a real estate investment. The books recommended in the appendices discuss this topic. Investopedia.com also has a good explanation of the concept. See investopida.com/articles/11/calculate-roi-real-estate.

    ○ To find a free on line calculator to help determine the rate of return on a property, go to calcxml.com/calculators/inv04 or homes.yahoo.com/calculators/investment

# 6. GUIDELINES FOR INVESTORS, PART II

*"Train the tenant or the tenant will train you"*. John W. Schaub

*"Buying a rental property isn't solely a financial decision.*
*Be honest about how big a commitment owning a house*
*will really be"*. Tara Siegel Bernard, *New York Times*

- Do not be greedy. Offer market rent or slightly below-market rent to ensure the property is occupied.

- Screen and train tenants. It is better to have no tenant than the wrong tenant. Learn to be an excellent property manager. The goal is to get a good tenant who will never move and pay off your mortgage.

  ○ Join your local apartment managers association for resources and guidance.

  ○ Stay in contact with tenants and treat them well. Resolve disputes by discussion and negotiation. Avoid confrontation and litigation.

○ In the event you have an undesirable tenant, use "cash for keys" to get them to move. Evictions take time and cost money.

○ Professional management is costly but may be appropriate as your holdings increase in number.

● Protect yourself from liability. Consult your Agent about insurance options, including defense against legal claims.

● Avoid creative real estate transactions such as buying a home subject to the underlying financing unless each party has counsel and is sophisticated in real estate transactions. If you are tempted to buy a house creatively, that is, without paying off the existing financing at the time of purchase, think twice. If the seller feels they have been wronged, s/he may sue you. Plaintiff's attorneys pursue these claims with vigor. You do not want to spend a year or more defending yourself and paying legal fees.

# 7. CONDOS – *A MIXED BAG*

*"Condos are the canaries of the real estate market"*. John W. Schaub

*"Never get emotionally married to a deal. Maintain your objectivity, do all the analysis, and if it does not generate the economic returns you require, pass on it"*. Jorge Perez, CEO, The Related Group of Florida, largest Hispanic-owned business in the U. S.

- Good news: with prices typically lower than single family houses, condos, especially in entry-level neighborhoods, may have good cash flow even with home owner's association dues (HOA), taxes, and maintenance. Bad news: see below.

- Condos may be difficult to finance if the complex has a low owner-occupancy rate, poor HOA financial status, a pending special assessment, and no FHA certification.

- Litigation may scare lenders and require all cash buyers—driving down the supply of buyers and the price of the home.

- Condominiums are a complex, restrictive form of ownership, with Homeowner Association Boards of Directors, as well as Covenants, Conditions and Restrictions (CC&Rs). Some who buy condos later regret the purchase because of tension and conflict with HOA boards.

- Condos are at their highest and best use. Improvements are limited to interior cosmetic upgrades.

- The inventory of condos in most cities is typically large relative to single-family homes. Condos are typically the "canaries of the market," that is, the first to drop in value in a market downturn.

- It may be more difficult to keep tenants in small condos long-term. As a result, you may need to spend money every time a tenant moves. Tenants are more likely to stay long-term in single family homes.

# 8. TAX BENEFITS OF INVESTMENT REAL ESTATE

*"Don't use taxes as an excuse for making a bad
real estate deal".* Leonard Baron, CPA

● *Have a good tax adviser on your team.* Investors, unlike owner
occupants, can deduct losses on real property. The following are
some of the rules:

○ Rental income is taxed at ordinary rates. Investors may be
able to deduct up to $25K in losses, including depreciation
*if* the owner has substantial involvement in managing the
property.

○ Depreciation: Take the value of home (not the land) and
divide by 27.5; deduct that amount each year against your
ordinary income up to $25K. Deductions are phased out if
the owner earns between $100K and $150K per year. As a
result, an owner may be able to post a tax loss even if generating a profit.

- ○ The depreciation is recaptured when selling the home. That is, at the time of sale, you pay a flat 25 percent rate on the amount depreciated. Exceptions: if you exchange the house for another property (called a 1031 exchange) or keep the house until you die, you pay no tax. Heirs inherit the rental at current market value and pay no tax on the gain.

- Real estate professionals—in a special category—can deduct 100 percent of real estate losses against ordinary income *regardless of how high their income:*

  - ○ Real estate professionals are defined as people who spend more than half their time each year working in a real property business and more than 751 hours a year in such business.

  - ○ A real property business includes property development, redevelopment, construction, reconstruction, acquisition, conversion, rental, operation, management, leasing, or a brokerage business.

  - ○ *Beware*: it is virtually impossible to qualify as a real estate professional if you have full-time employment outside of real estate.

# 9. CONSIDER SHORT SALES AND FORECLOSURES

*"Buy the neighborhood not the house. Select the best neighborhood you can afford. Then select a house in the lower or middle end of the price range in that neighborhood".* Rob Zache, President, Central Place Real Estate, Madison, Wisconsin

- Foreclosed homes, known as REOs (real estate owned), are for experienced, more sophisticated buyers:

    O  They may be cheaper but often have multiple offers.

    O  Property can be in poor condition.

    O  All cash may get your offer accepted.

    O  Property is sold without warranty.

    O  Seller – the bank - makes no disclosures in CA.

    O  Transaction can close quickly.

    O  Lender's purchase agreement is seller/bank friendly.

- O The buyers may lose their earnest money deposit if they do not close.

- ● Short sales (home has negative equity, that is, debt against the home is greater than the home's market value and lender accepts short payoff.) are for patient buyers:

- O The property is typically in better condition.

- O Seller in CA is required to make full disclosures regarding property condition.

- O The average short sale takes about five to six months to close. All cash is not as important. Short sales sell for market value or a bit below market value. Homes are sold "as is."

- O The California Association of Realtors Residential Purchase Agreement (RPA) is buyer friendly; assuming buyer does not release their contingencies, their earnest money deposit should be returned in the event the buyer does not close escrow.

# 10. SHOULD YOU BUY HOUSES AT A TRUSTEE'S SALE*?

*"Getting a good deal can be dangerous. Nothing beats knowing what you are doing"*. James M. Allen, Esq., President & General Counsel, Action Foreclosure Services, Inc., La Mesa, CA

- I occasionally receive phone calls from real estate investors in a state of panic. The typical fact pattern: Investor purchased a home at a trustee's sale. Market value of home was $500,000, and investor paid $200,000. Wow! Investor thought they got a deal. Subsequently, they learn the home had a first trust deed in the amount of $500,000 and that they purchased a $500K home for $700K not $200K. Not such a good deal! They are now responsible for the first trust deed! What can the investor do? Answer: Investor is out of luck!

- Jim Allen, Esq., who has been involved in trustee's sales as a trustee, bidder, expert witness, and counsel to bidders, trustees, and lenders for nearly forty years, commented as follows:

○ "Carelessness in investigating the status of the property, the title, condition, possession and the like can be costly.

○ "When you buy a property in the ordinary course, you negotiate, have an escrow, get to make inspections, examine title, look for termites, get a homeowner's warranty, have some time to know what you are getting, even consult your lawyer, not that anybody actually does that. None of those protections are available when bidding at a trustee's sale. It can be very dangerous to get a good deal.

○ "We had a young man show up at one of our sales a few years ago, the only bidder, who outbid the lender. We gave him his deed and cashed his checks. He thought he was buying a house worth $500-600,000 for $176,000.

○ "A few months later he called back to ask, *"Did you know about another deed of trust on that property?"* It turned out he asked a title company friend who told him there was another trust deed but that it had probably been conveyed back to the owner. Well, it wasn't. Buyer bought a house worth $500-600,000 for about $700,000, and Bank of America subsequently foreclosed on him.

○ "If you are the only bidder at a sale that seems like a steal, it pays to ask yourself why you are so lucky all of a sudden".

● Bottom line: If you want to be a real estate investor, follow Jim's advice: Do not buy houses sold at trustee sales, *unless you know what you are doing.*

● *California is a quick foreclosure state; foreclosures are typically done by a trustee's sale which takes as little as four months. In a judicial foreclosure state, Florida, New York, and New Jersey, for example, a lender must file a law suit against a borrower in default, and the foreclosure process can take a year or longer.

- If you are interested in how foreclosures are conducted state by state, see http://en.wikipedia.org/wiki/Foreclosure; http://www.realtytrac.com/foreclosure-laws/foreclosure-laws-comparison.asp; or http://www.propertyradar.com/foreclosure-guides/fore-closure-101/non-judicial-foreclosure-process.

# 11. SHORT SALE SUCCESS FACTORS – *TIPS FOR BUYERS*

*"Be prepared to close your brief case and walk away"*. Bart Wolstein, Cleveland real estate developer and philanthropist

- Buyers should look for several factors to achieve a successful transaction:

  O A listing agent with substantial short sale experience and a successful track record closing short sales.

  O An owner in financial distress who stopped making payments at about the same time the house was listed on the Multiple Listing Service.

  O A house in good condition with only one lien. Avoid multiple liens, especially judgment liens, state tax liens, or IRS liens. (It is not impossible to close a short sale with these issues. It can be a great deal more challenging, however, and it is especially important to have an experienced realtor working on the file.)

○ A borrower/seller who did not refinance and take money out beyond the purchase price. Short sales are easier if the original purchase money loans are in place.

● Two more tips for buyers:

○ Have your realtor search the multiple listing service for "short sale approved." (The phrase may not be used in all areas or by all listing agents.) This is when an offer was accepted by the seller, the bank approved the short sale, and the buyer cancelled. Make an offer! If your offer is accepted, you may be able to close quickly.

○ Search the MLS for "contingent listings," (may not be used in all areas) meaning an offer has been accepted by the seller pending lender approval. Make a "back-up" offer! You may have a good chance of closing because the current buyer may cancel.

# 12. IDEAL SHORT SALE BUYERS

*"Real estate entrepreneurs too often fall in love with deals". Scott A. Wolstein, CEO, Developers Diversified Realty, Puerto Rico*

- The ideal short sale buyer exhibits the following characteristics:

  O They are pre-approved for a loan.

  O They understand that the sale is "as is."

  O They put few or no contingencies in their offer.

  O They are patient and can wait to close.

  O They have the resources to make needed repairs or contribute to a lien payoff if necessary.

  O They understand that the lender will sell the home at or near market value.

- Although a buyer may be able to negotiate with the short sale bank, s/he must understand that the lender will make the final call on terms, closing date, and price.

# 13. DUE DILIGENCE IN HIRING A BUYER'S REALTOR

*"My best real estate advice sounds simple. Find a real estate professional you can trust. I mean really trust".*
John Bearden, CEO, GMAC Home Services

- A good, experienced realtor can make the process of buying much easier and less stressful. Some realtors specialize in assisting investor clients. They may have the ability to calculate the return on investment on a property and also keep tabs on the market— constantly looking for appropriate properties for you.

- Questions to ask a realtor: What is your experience? How many transactions have you handled? What is your education and background? Do you own investment property? Does your office have in house counsel to assist you?

- Beware: If you are going to be a real estate investor, you must do your own due diligence before buying any property. You cannot rely on your realtor to do that for you. Recommended reading: Professor Leonard Baron's book "Real Estate Ownership, Investment and Due Diligence 101".

# EPILOGUE

*"There is no good excuse for anybody not to retire a millionaire"*.
Matthew Allen, author "How to Get Rich for Dummies"

As a young FBI Agent, I had the opportunity to conduct background investigations regarding attorneys and state judges who were applicants for federal judgeships. In my experience, poor money management skills were the number one reason why these individuals did not receive a judicial appointment.

*The lesson for all of us*: Whatever your education, occupation, and life's work, before you spend money you do not have, before you buy a house you cannot afford, before you do anything, develop an overall financial plan. Practice smart money management and put your financial house in order. You do not want to find down the road that your failure to plan harmed your family, your ability to get the job or promotion you wanted, or denied you the retirement you deserve. Ask yourself: Where will you be when your working years come to an end? Living a Spartan existence on a social security annuity or living the best years of your life? You decide.

Recommended reading: "For Retirees, a Million Dollar Illusion", Jeff Sommer, *New York Times,* June 8, 2013

# APPENDICES

A. What Gary's Parents Taught Him about Money

B. What John Wesley Taught All of Us about Money

C. What You Should Teach Your Kids about Money

D. Bear and Bull Markets Defined

E. The Dark Side of Bonds

F. Recommended Reading

G. Twenty Signs You Might Live to 100

H. Annuities

I. Reverse Mortgages – The Loan of Last Resort

J. VA Loans

K. Price-to-Rent Ratios

L. Index Funds: Definition & Comments

M. Index Funds vs. Exchange Traded Funds (ETFs)

N. Index Funds vs. Hedge Funds

# A. WHAT GARY'S PARENTS TAUGHT HIM ABOUT MONEY

*Live below your means; save and invest regularly*

*"As a parent, the best way to teach kids about finances is to be a role model".* Edward Powell, chief consumer officer, LendingTree.com

- Gary's parents were kids during the Great Depression in the 1930s, and their experiences made them distrustful of Wall Street, the stock market and banks. They saw banks fail and many families lose their life savings.

- Gary's parents paid cash for everything they purchased. They lived within their means, did not spend money they did not have, never used credit cards, and paid cash for their cars. They also gave modestly to their church and charity.

- They purchased a four-unit apartment building in St. Paul, Minnesota, Gary's home town; the tenants paid the mortgage, and his family lived rent free. Gary's dad religiously purchased government bonds every payday; he started to save and invest in his twenties.

- His parents "could not afford" to send him to a private college; as a result, he attended the University of Minnesota, a public university, and enrolled in Army ROTC. He received a check each month to cover his tuition and other expenses. Gary used the G.I. Bill to pay for law school.

- Gary's parents retired at a young age to a golf course community in Arizona, paying cash for their new home, buying a new car with cash every three to four years, and living comfortably the rest of their lives. They continued to be active in and contribute to their church.

# B. WHAT JOHN WESLEY TAUGHT ALL OF US ABOUT MONEY

*"What should rise is not the Christian's standard of living but the standard of giving"*. John Wesley

- The books of Judaism, Christianity, and Islam contain advice and guidance on money management and financial planning. The Bible alone contains two thousand verses on budgeting, debt, saving, investing, wealth, and giving. Seventy-five percent of the parables of Jesus deal with money.

- John Wesley, 18th century Christian theologian and co-founder of the Methodist Movement, was known for following three principles: *"Gain all you can, save all you can, and give all you can."*

- Wesley practiced the *"give all you can"* principle, setting and maintaining the same modest standard of living throughout his life. Even when Wesley earned many times more than required to maintain his minimal standard of living, he continued to live modestly and give the rest away.

- Wesley's reading of the Bible led him to conclude that Christians should:

  O Take care of their family;

  O Be content with what they have;

  O Deal honorably with others, even with the unscrupulous;

  O Avoid debt;

  O Look for opportunity to give to others and serve your community.

# C. WHAT YOU SHOULD TEACH YOUR KIDS ABOUT MONEY

*"I would as soon leave my son a curse as the almighty dollar".*
Andrew Carnegie, 1835 -1919, business magnate and philanthropist
with a net worth of $298.3 billion in 2007 dollars, *Forbes* magazine

- Kids don't learn financial literacy at school; parents have the greatest influence on a child's financial literacy skills.

- Give kids unconditional love—don't give them "stuff." Teach them to save and invest at an early age. Let them do odd jobs around the house; children benefit from earning money, making budgets, saving and spending wisely.

- Talk to your kids about money. Share with them the family's financial challenges. Do not keep them in the dark.

- Teach them to *"Give, Save, Spend."* Read the *"Three Cups,"* by Tony Townsley:

○ Tony and his wife developed the idea of the "Three Cups." They wrote a wonderful book for parents about the lessons in life and money for their son Jake.

○ Jake's weekly allowance, starting at age 5, was divided into three cups—one cup was for giving, one for saving, and one cup was for spending.

○ If Jake wanted something, he had to save to buy it; he was not given "stuff" by his parents. Jake learned to give, save, and spend.

- *Gifting money makes people financially inept; if adult children cannot afford a house, do not cosign for their mortgages.*

- *Recommended reading*: "How to Teach Kids About Investing", Aparna Navayanan, *Wall Street Journal,* August 1, 2013

# D. BEAR AND BULL MARKETS DEFINED

Thanks to Investopedia.com

*"Bear markets (falling markets) make people a lot of money. They just don't know it at the time". Warren Buffet*

*Bear Markets*: A market condition in which the prices of securities are falling, and widespread pessimism causes negative sentiment to be self-sustaining. As investors anticipate losses and selling continues, pessimism grows. Although figures can vary, for many, a downturn of 20 percent or more in multiple broad market indexes, such as the Dow Jones Industrial Average (DJIA) or Standard & Poor's 500 Index (S&P 500), over at least a two-month period, is considered entry into a bear market.

*Bull Markets*: A market condition characterized by optimism, investor confidence, and expectations that strong results will continue. It's difficult to predict consistently when the trends in the market will change. Part of the difficulty is that psychological effects and speculation may sometimes play a large role in the markets.

The use of "bull" and "bear" to describe markets comes from the way the animals attack their opponents. A bull thrusts its horns up into the air while a bear swipes its paws down. These actions are metaphors for the movement of a market. If the trend is up, it's a bull market. If the trend is down, it's a bear market.

# E. THE DARK SIDE
# OF BONDS

Comments by Dennis Muckermann, co-founder,
Alexander & Muckermann, San Diego, CA

- Bonds suffer from default risk by the issuer. The fixed terms of bonds may be changed or reduced by negotiation or government action.

- The capital raised by selling bonds is hardly ever paid off. Bonds are refinanced or rolled over until the debt is reduced by inflation or defaulted on because of financial or government risks.

- Bonds are subject to interest rate risk. Especially now when interest rates are at historic lows, the price of bonds will fall when interest rates increase. Their price cannot increase significantly because interest rates are too low to drop much further.

- In studying the long-term outlook for companies that issued bonds in the past, most, if not all, components of the Dow Jones Industrial average in 1900 do not exist today.

- The overall reality is that bonds offer only a relatively low and fixed return if everything in the future goes according to plan but are subject to many and varied risks that can decimate both the principal and income.

- Bonds don't yield enough to cover the risks and in the long run are poor investments.

- There is no perfect investment. All investments are subject to risk.

## Comment

Few investment professionals would recommend a portfolio with no bonds. *Review* Chapter 11, "Six Guidelines to Successful Investing" for a discussion on the role of bonds in your portfolio, as well as other options to buffer the short term volatility of stocks, for example, a money market fund. You decide what role bonds should play in your portfolio, if any.

# F. RECOMMENDED READING

*Money Management & Financial Planning*

- *The Financial Stewardship Bible* published by the American Bible Society. The Bible contains over two thousand verses on budgeting, debt, saving, investing, wealth, and giving. In this version all money management and financial planning verses are highlighted in green.

- *The Millionaire Next Door,* by Stanley and Danko

- *Total Money Makeover,* Dave Ramsey, host of Dave Ramsey show

## *Investing*

- *Think & Grow Rich,* Napoleon Hill—a classic; one of the best-selling books of all time

- *The Richest Man in Babylon*, George S. Clason – a classic

- *All Your Worth*, Elizabeth Warren & Amelia Warren Tyagi

- *The Little Book of Common Sense Investing*, John C. Bogle

- *Investing Made Simple*, Mike Piper

- *How a Second Grader Beats Wall Street*, Alan S. Roth

- *Millionaire Teacher*, Andrew Hallam

- *I Will Teach You to be Rich*, Ramit Sethi

## Investing in Real Estate

- *How I Turned $1,000 into a Million in My Spare Time*, William Nickerson

- *Private Real Estate Investing - Part I, The Basics*, Roger J. Brown, PhD

- *Real Estate Ownership, Investment and Due Diligence 101*, Leonard Baron, MBA, CPA

- *Building Wealth One House at a Time*, John W. Schaub

# G. TWENTY SIGNS YOU MIGHT LIVE TO 100*

*Do Not Outlive Your Money*

(*Mind Body Sole magazine, fall 2010)

- You eat purple food.

- You have been a college freshman.

- You have a drama-free marriage.

- You enjoy good friendships.

- You have strong legs.

- You set goals.

- You feel 13 years younger than you are.

- You have a positive outlook.

- You're outgoing.

- You have skinny friends.

- You don't have a housekeeper.

- You often walk instead of drive.

- You do aerobic activity five hours a week.

- You don't like burgers.

- You skip cola, including diet.

- You love tea.

- You limit calories to 1400 to 2000 a day.

- You don't snore.

- You were not overweight as a teen.

- You have a flat belly.

# H. ANNUITIES

*An Immediate Annuity May Make Sense*

- An annuity is an insurance product. They allow you to avoid two retirement risks:

  1. That a stock market crash will decimate your savings.

  2. That you will outlive your money.

- For example, a man age 65 with a $200K contribution can get $800 per month for life; a woman age 65 with $200K contribution can get $740 per month for life.

- The amount you receive is based on interest rates in effect at the time you buy the annuity. Today's rates are low; as a result, you may want to wait to consider an annuity until rates go up.

- Upon your death, the balance of your initial contribution goes to the insurance company—not your estate.

- Commissions on annuities can be high. Find out from your company what the commission is before you buy—shop and compare.

- More savers may get access to annuities. New proposed government rules will provide that employers can give an annuity option in 401K retirement plans.

## Inflation Adjusted Annuities Are Available

- You can buy an inflation-adjusted annuity through Vanguard, the mutual fund company.

- For $400,000 a 65-year-old man could receive a monthly initial payment of $1,552 to $1,677, depending on the insurer.

- The payment would be adjusted for inflation each year. Payments would stop at death; the insurance company keeps any balance.

## How Annuities Are Taxed?

- Brad Dewan, San Diego tax attorney, answered this question as follows:

- Each annuity payment is split between a "return of principal" and "income." The concept: the money is invested and earns "returns" over time, and each payment has a component of these "earnings."

- The annuity company projects that the annuity payments over time will be split between "principal" (not taxable) and "earnings" (taxable).

- The "return of principal" is split over the remaining life expectancy of the buyer.

## Social Security is an Annuity
### *Wait to Buy More Coverage*

- An *annuity* pays a guaranteed income for life.

- With social security, the longer you wait, the greater your monthly benefits will be when you get payments.

  O  If you wait from 62 until 66, payments go up by 33 percent.

  O  If you wait until 70, benefits go up by at least 75 percent.

  O  So, waiting is the easiest way to buy more annuity coverage; few take advantage of this:

  O  Currently, 46 percent begin claiming at 62, the first year eligible.

  O  Less than 5 percent delay past age 66.

- Recommended reading: "Bolstering Your Benefits" by Kelly Green, *Wall Street Journal*, March 15, 2013

# I. REVERSE MORTGAGES –
# *THE LOAN OF LAST RESORT*

*"Fine print on reverse mortgages snares many"*. Kenneth Harney, columnist for the Washington Post Writers Group

*"The problem is that almost by definition people who take out reverse mortgages are in financial distress,"* Anthony Webb, Boston College

- You can now apply for a reverse mortgage at the age of 62. Nearly 50 percent now apply under the age of 70. This early age raises the danger that the owners could out-live the money they receive from the reverse mortgage.

- Beware of scammer con artist salespeople who take advantage of the elderly. Beware of huge costs associated with reverse mortgages.

- If the borrower does not pay property taxes and insurance on the home, s/he may lose the home to foreclosure.

- If the signer dies, the non-signing spouses may lose the home to foreclosure. Thus, if a couple decide to obtain a reverse mortgage, both should sign the loan documents.

- An alternative to a reverse mortgage might be to downsize, sell the home, take the equity, and buy another home free and clear.

## Reverse Mortgage Details

You will find substantial information concerning reverse mortgages on line. An excellent source is AARP.org. We also recommend www.hud.gov.

Reverse mortgages are increasing in popularity with seniors who have equity in their homes and want to supplement their income. The only reverse mortgage insured by the U.S. Federal Government is called a Home Equity Conversion Mortgage or HECM, and is only available through an FHA approved lender. To get answers to frequently asked questions about HUD's reverse mortgages go to hud.gov.

Recommended reading: "Reverse-Mortgage Redo" by Anne Tergesen in *The Wall Street Journal*, February 10, 2013; "Reverse Mortgages: Still Worth the Risk?"; Carole Fleck, aarp.org/bulletin, April 2013; "Rules for Reverse Mortgages May Become More Restrictive", Tara Siegel Bernard, *New York Times,* July 12, 201.

Kenneth Harney, quoted above, has written a number of articles on reverse mortgages. All are available on line.

# J. VA LOANS

*Contributed by Ken Bates, Military Home Loans, San Diego*
*Thanks Ken!*

The VA guidelines say the following regarding Debt-To-Income: "A ratio greater than 41 percent requires close scrutiny unless: residual income exceeds the guideline by at least 20%." Residual income is a budget methodology, subtracting known expenses from income to see what remains for life (the required residual income). While it accounts for region and family size, it applies the same required residual income regardless of the income level of the buyer. In contrast, a Debt-To-Income ratio assumes with a higher income a borrower will need more money for life items. For high income earners, it's possible to exceed the residual income required by 20% with a DTI that's in excess of 60%. This loan would meet VA guidelines.

Because of this and to maintain consistency and risk mitigation, most lenders will apply their own maximum Debt-To-Income ratios to VA loans. Many lenders will go up to 50% Debt-To-Income on a "solid" file, and over 50% on a case by case basis when there are compensating factors. But each lender is allowed to make their own determination of where they want to stop as long as they're consistent with all their borrowers. This is why a buyer can be approved by three different lenders for the exact same VA loan, with the exact same income and debts numbers, and be told three different pre-approval amounts.

Considering nearly 88% of buyers using VA do so with a zero down payment, it would be expected that the default rate would be noticeable higher than FHA where at least 3.5% down payment is needed (both are full documentation loans, back by the government, and use similar underwriting criteria). However, the opposite is true, with VA having a significantly lower default rate, thus defying the notion that more 'skin in the game' makes for a lower risk loan. Without any tangible reason for this, the conclusion drawn by most observers is borrowers using VA are more committed to seeing their obligations through to the end. In essence, it's a character and integrity issue military members live day in and day out; manifesting itself in the lower default rate.

Check out pages 62-66 of this for where my 88% number comes from and other info you might find helpful (especially the 4th link for default rate discussion):

http://www.vba.va.gov/REPORTS/abr/2011_abr.pdf

http://www.va.gov/vetdata/docs/Quickfacts/Stats_at_a_glance_FINAL.pdf

http://www.va.gov/opa/pressrel/pressrelease.cfm?id=2400

http://www.va.gov/opa/pressrel/pressrelease.cfm?id=2255

# K. PRICE-TO-RENT RATIOS

*Wikipedia.com*

Definition of Price-to-Rent Ratio

A mathematical calculation utilized in the Trulia.com rent versus buy index that compares the totals costs of homeownership with the total cost of renting a similar property. The total costs of homeownership considered by the ratio include:

- Mortgage principal and interest

- Property taxes

- Insurance

- Closing costs

- HOA dues where appropriate

- Mortgage insurance where appropriate

## *Investopedia.com*

The price-to-rent ratio provides a comparison between owning and renting properties in certain cities. The ratio uses the average list price with average yearly rent on two-bedroom apartments, condos and town-homes that are listed on www.trulia.com, a real estate search website. The price-to-rent ratio is calculated by dividing the average list price by the average yearly rent price, as follows: Price-to-rent ratio = Average list price / (Average Rent * 12)

Trulia.com establishes thresholds for the ratios as follows:

- Price-to-rent ratio of 1 to 15 = much better to buy than rent

- Price-to-rent ratio of 16 to 20 = typically better to rent than buy

- Price-to-rent ratio of 21 or more = much better to rent than buy

See http://www.zillowblog.com/research/2012/11/27/in-most-of-u-s-buying-still-beats-renting-after-only-three-years/

# L. INDEX FUNDS: DEFINITION & COMMENTS

*Investopdia.com explains index fund*

An index fund is a type of mutual fund with a portfolio constructed to match or track the components of a market index, such as the Standard & Poor's 500 Index (S&P 500). An index mutual fund is said to provide broad market exposure, low operating expenses and low portfolio turnover.

## *Investopida.com explains indexing*

"Indexing" is a passive form of fund management that has been successful in outperforming most actively managed mutual funds. While the most popular index funds track the S&P 500, a number of other indexes, including the Russell 2000 (small companies), the DJ Wilshire 5000 (total stock market), the MSCI EAFE (foreign stocks in Europe, Australasia, Far East) and the Lehman Aggregate Bond Index (total bond market) are widely used for index funds.

Investing in an index fund is a form of passive investing. The primary advantage to such a strategy is the lower management expense ratio on an index fund. Also, a majority of actively managed mutual funds fail to beat broad indexes, such as the S&P 500.

## Comments about Index Funds

"The Index Fund Wins Again", Mark Hulbert,
*New York Times*, February 21, 2013

"THERE'S yet more evidence that it makes sense to invest in simple, plain-vanilla index funds whose low fees often lead to better net returns than hedge funds and actively managed mutual with more impressive performance numbers.

"Basic stock market index funds generally aspire to nothing more than matching the returns of a market benchmark. So in a miserable year for stocks, index funds may not look very appealing. But it turns out that, after fees and taxes, it is the extremely rare actively managed fund or hedge fund that does better than a simple index fund".

Quoting Mark Kritzman, CEO, Windham Capital Management of Boston: "It is very hard, if not impossible to justify active management for most individual, taxable investors, if their goal is to grow wealth". Those who still insist on an actively managed fund are almost certainly "deluding themselves".

# M. INDEX FUNDS VS. EXCHANGE TRADED FUNDS (ETFS)

*"Given the comparison of costs, the average passive retail investor will decide to go with index funds".* Leonard Kostovetsky, PhD in Economics, Princeton University

*Wikipedia.com*

An exchange-traded fund (ETF) is an investment fund traded on stock exchanges, much like stocks. An ETF holds assets such as stocks, commodities, or bonds, and trades close to its net asset value over the course of the trading day. Most ETFs track an index, such as a stock index or bond index. ETFs may be attractive as investments because of their low costs, tax efficiency, and stock-like features.

## *Investopdia.com*

Given the increased popularity of exchange-traded funds (ETFs), you would think that index investors have fallen in love with this investment vehicle. Even though ETFs have only been around since 1993 (whereas the first index mutual fund was introduced in 1975), by the end of 2004 their total net assets amounted to almost half those of index funds.

Typically, the choice between ETFs and index funds will come down to the most important issues: management fees, shareholder transaction costs, taxation and other qualitative differences.

According to Leonard Kostovetsky*, a comparison of the costs favors index funds as the choice for most passive retail investors. See "Index Mutual Funds and Exchange Traded Funds", published in the *Journal of Portfolio Management, 2003.*

*PhD in Economics, Princeton University, Assistant Professor of Economics, Simon Graduate School of Business, University of Rochester

Leonard Kostovetsky: "If you were looking at a holding period of one year, you would be required to hold over $60,000 of an ETF for the management fee and taxation savings to offset the transaction costs. With a longer-term time horizon of 10 years, the break-even point would be lowered to $13,000. However, both these limits are usually out of range for the average retail investor.

"As with many financial decisions, determining which investment vehicle to commit to comes down to "dollars and cents." *Given the comparison of costs, the average passive retail investor will decide to go with index funds. For these investors, keeping it simple can be the best policy.* Passive institutional investors and active traders, on the other hand, will likely be swayed by qualitative factors in making their decision. Be sure you know where you stand before you commit".

# N. INDEX FUNDS VS. HEDGE FUNDS

*"If history is any guide, you will be better off investing in low-cost index funds"*. Mark Hulbert, Wall Street Journal, May 31, 2013

*"Hedge Funds - definition: The rich stealing from the rich"*. Andrew Hallam, author, "Millionaire Teacher"

- "For the most part, hedge funds (unlike mutual funds) are unregulated because they cater to sophisticated investors. In the U.S., laws require that the majority of investors in the fund be accredited. That is, they must earn a minimum amount of money annually and have a net worth of more than $1 million, along with a significant amount of investment knowledge. You can think of hedge funds as mutual funds for the super- rich. They are similar to mutual funds in that investments are pooled and professionally managed, but differ in that the fund has far more flexibility in its investment strategies". Investopedia.com

- *Accredited investor*: In the U. S., an individual - to be considered an accredited investor - must have a net worth of at least one million dollars - not including the value of the primary residence - or have income of at least $200,000 each year for the last two years and expectations to make the same amount in the current year. Wikipedia.com

- Recommended reading: "The Verdict Is In: Hedge Funds aren't Worth the Money", Mark Hulbert, *Wall Street Journal*, May 31, 2013. In the article Hulbert makes a number of points, including:

  O Hedge funds charge high fees – typically 2% of assets and 20% of profits.

  O Hedge funds supposedly pursue complicated strategies that do well whether markets are going up or down.

  O The average hedge fund has done no better than the stock market since the October 2007 bull-market high.

  O According to David Hsieh, Duke University, the proportion of hedge funds making enough to justify their high fees is small; it is nearly impossible to identify in advance the select few hedge fund managers who add value.

  O *The investment lesson that emerges: Invest in index funds.* Among the lowest cost ways to invest in the stock and bond markets are the Vanguard Total Stock Market Index Fund, which charges an expense ratio of 0.17% or $17.00 per $10,000 invested, and the Vanguard Total Bond Market Index Fund, which charges 0.2% or $20.00 per $10,000 invested.

# ACKNOWLEDGMENTS

While we would like to take credit for the information and ideas in this book, we must acknowledge sources of information and those who came before us. We are in debt to many – parents (see "What Gary's Parent's Taught Him about Money" in the Appendices), family, teachers, professors, advisers, clients, authors, journalists, and fellow attorneys in San Diego, *The Wall Street Journal*, and *The New York Times*, as well as the many borrowers who contacted us over the years. We have attempted to identify individual sources where appropriate and have shared with you our favorite investment books in the Appendices.

Thanks to Jennifer Manganello, Esq., bankruptcy attorney, Dory Laramore, financial writer, and Andrew Sussman, Esq., tax and estate planning attorney, who read and took the time to write their thoughts about our book.

Thanks to Dennis Muckermann, co-founder, Alexander & Muckermann, Inc. See Appendices F, "The Dark Side of Bonds." Thanks to Ken Bates, Military Home Loan Programs, San Diego. See Appendices K, "VA Mortgage Loan Guidelines." Thanks to Michael and Andrea who contributed "Case Study: Couple Discuss Financial Planning & Money Management".

Thanks also to a number of colleagues who allowed us to quote them in the text: Jim Allen, Esq., Roger Brown, PhD, Larry Branton, Esq., Brad Dewan, Esq., Fred Holsman, Guild Mortgage, Dory Laramore, Richard Steiner, Esq., Leonard Baron, CPA and MBA, Thomas D. Rutledge, Esq., and my brother Lyle. Thanks to Robert Plotkin, retired foreign- service officer, U. S. Department of State, Roger Brown, PhD, Larry Branton, Esq., David Amack, former English teacher, and my brother Lyle for taking the time to read a draft and give us suggestions to improve the book. Robert Plotkin, currently President of Celsius Group, San Diego, also contributed to the book's title. Thanks Bob!

Thanks to the *U–T San Diego*, the daily newspaper of San Diego, CA. The paper carried public service announcements concerning a number of San Diego County Law Library seminars that I taught, thus allowing me to connect with many homeowners in the greater San Diego area. A special thanks to Lily Leung who covers residential real estate for the U-T. Lilly interviewed and quoted us on a number of occasions. Her many articles on local real estate developments kept us current on the San Diego market.

A *special* thanks to the many continuing legal education providers who invited me to speak at seminars and forums on the housing crisis. The classes gave me the opportunity to meet and connect with countless attorneys in San Diego, CA, and the U. S. Without the many referrals from lawyers and the opportunity to counsel distressed homeowners, this book would not have been written. The organizations and individuals include:

- San Diego County Bar Association: The bar went all out to support our efforts to train and recruit attorneys to counsel homeowners in financial distress at San Diego area HOME Clinics. Thanks to Ellen Miller-Sharp, Executive Director, bar Presidents Heather Rosing, Jerrilyn Malana, and Dan Link, as well as chairs or co- chairs of the Real Property Law Section, Justin White, Houston Watson, Scott Miller, Todd Bulich (my co-chair) and Elizabeth Smith-Chavez.

- San Diego County Law Library: The law library invited me to teach countless legal education classes on the housing crisis and foreclosure issues, promoting the classes to both attorneys and the community at large. The classes allowed me to meet and connect with many attorneys and homeowners. Thanks to John Adkins, Library Director, Cheryl Weeks Fry, Assistant Director, Isabel Eustaquio, attorney and continuing legal education chair, Debra Morse, attorney and branch manager, Vista, Benita Ghura, attorney and branch manager, Chula Vista, Kelly Keach, attorney, main branch, and Amanda Mongolo, paralegal main branch.

- Judge Advocate General's Corp in San Diego County: The many JAG officers in San Diego referred many active duty and retired military people to me in the last four years. A special thanks to Harris Brumer, Director of Legal Assistance at Marine Corps Air Station Miramar. Mr. Brumer invited me to speak on numerous occasions at both Miramar and Camp Pendleton, thus introducing me to countless JAG officers over the years.

- The Housing Opportunities Collaborative, sponsor of the HOME Clinics in San Diego County: The Collaborative gave me the opportunity to mentor and train area attorneys on housing and foreclosure issues, as well as counsel distressed homeowners. Thanks to San Diego attorney Myrna Pascual, founder of the HOME Clinics, and "Vino" Pajanor, Executive Director. A special thanks to attorney Shanna Welsh. Shanna was diligent in attending my classes and volunteering at almost every clinic over a number of years. In fact, she has now taken my position as liaison between the Collaborative and the county bar association. The clinics, she said, gave her the experience and confidence to start her own law practice.

- North County Bar, Real Property Law Section (RPLS): The RPLS of the North County Bar in San Diego invited me on a number of occasions to speak at legal education seminars and/or to organize training sessions for attorneys on the housing crisis. As a result, I was able to meet and connect with attorneys in the north county of San Diego and assist them and their clients with housing issues. Thanks to section chairs James Lund, Joseph Stine, and Deborah Zoller.

- Christian Legal Society, San Diego Chapter: A special thanks to past presidents John Yphantides, Jennifer Patrick and current president David Hallett, as well as board members Miles Lawrence, Larry Dershem, and Eric Peterson for inviting me to speak at several of their meetings on the housing crisis and related legal issues.

- The City of Chula Vista: Thanks to City Attorney Glen Googins for organizing a forum on the housing crisis and inviting me to speak, thus allowing me to connect with numerous homeowners in Chula Vista, CA.

- San Diego Elder Law & Advocacy: The attorneys in this office provide legal assistance to the elder population in San Diego. Thanks to supervising attorney Jaime Levine and staff attorneys Bob Martin, Karin Schumacher and Sharon Lee for inviting me to speak at their office, thus allowing me to meet and connect with their legal staff.

- La Jolla Bar Association: Thanks to President Virginia Gaburo for inviting me to speak at one of their meetings, thus allowing me to connect with numerous attorneys who live and/or practice in La Jolla, CA.

- The State Bar of CA: Special thanks to attorney George Hurley, member, Executive Committee, Real Property Law Section, State Bar of CA. George invited both me and Vikki to speak at the State Bar's Annual Meeting in Monterey, CA, in September 2012, thus allowing us to meet and connect with numerous attorneys throughout CA. Joining us on the panel was San Diego tax attorney Brad Dewan.

- Legal Aid Society of San Diego, Inc.: The Legal Aid Society is a committed and compassionate group of legal professionals dedicated to providing equal access to justice for the poor through aggressive, quality legal services. Special thanks to Sara Raffer Lee, pro bono program manager, senior staff attorneys Allyson Snow, Richard Steiner and lead housing attorney Bernadette Probus.

- Earl Gilliam Bar Association: A special thanks to attorney Omar Passons, president- elect, who invited me on several occasions to speak at community forums concerning the housing crisis, thus giving me the opportunity to connect with homeowners in San Diego. (The Earl Gilliam Bar Association is named after San Diego's first black federal judge, the late Earl Gilliam. As an FBI Agent, I had the honor of conducting his background investigation before he was appointed to the federal bench.)

- Chicago Title, San Diego, CA: A special thanks to Fred Eckert, Assistant Vice President. Fred gives back to the community in many ways. At Chicago Title, he organized seminars on mortgage and housing crisis issues and invited me and Vikki to speak at many programs, thus allowing us to meet many homeowners in San Diego.

- San Diego area law schools: Thanks to adjunct professors Duane Horning, USD, Todd Bulich, California Western, Lilys MC Coy, Director, Solo Practice Program, Thomas Jefferson School of Law, and Kyle Yeage, alumni/graduate, California Western for inviting me to speak at their law schools.

- National Business Institute: NBI – nbi-sems.com – is the largest provider of continuing legal education classes in the United States. Vikki, Brad Dewan, San Diego tax attorney, and I have been presenting three to four seminars each year since approximately 2008 to hundreds of attorneys and paralegals. As a result, we connected with many legal professionals throughout the nation. A special thanks to Jonathan Cook and Julie Weinkauf. They are always a pleasure to work with. Thanks also to our colleague Brad Dewan, San Diego tax attorney. Brad initially invited us to join him and present the seminars as a panel. We have become a good team, teaching approximately twelve to fifteen NBI seminars over the last three to four years.

- Thanks also to a numerous other continuing legal education providers in the United States who invited me to speak at national webinars and seminars. Some videotaped my classes in San Diego. These CLE providers include attorneycredits.com, lawreviewcle.com, mylawcle.com, lexvid.com, and rossdalecle.com.

- Lastly, we acknowledge and thank the many homeowners who contacted us over the years, seeking information, guidance, direction and hope. We learned a great deal. Our message to those who contacted us: *Money problems are fixable. America is a country of second chances for everyone.*

# ABOUT THE AUTHORS

## Gary M. Laturno, Esq. – gary@landkrealty.com

- B. S., University of Minnesota; J.D., Loyola University, New Orleans

- Practiced law for 30 years; AV Rating Martindale Hubbell

- Named to Top Lawyers in San Diego, *San Diego Magazine,* 2013

- President & General Counsel, Laturno Kuick Realty, San Diego, California

- Of Counsel, Laturno & Graves, Escondido, CA

- Past Co-Chair, Real Property Law Section, San Diego County Bar Association,

- Member, Real Property, Taxation and Bankruptcy Law Sections, SDCBA

- Past Chair, Community Service Committee, SDCBA

- Former FBI Chief of Civil Litigation, FBI HQ, Washington, D. C.

- Former FBI Press Spokesman and Principal Legal Adviser, San Diego Division

- Arbitrator & Mediator, American Arbitration Association

- Mediator, San Diego Superior Court Mediation Panel

- Investor and property manager for 25 years

- Counseled over 2,000 homeowners in financial distress since 2007

- Mediated foreclosure disputes with the nation's largest mortgage lenders

- Featured speaker at California and national continuing legal education seminars including the California State Bar Annual Meeting, Monterey, CA

# Victoria K. Kuick, MBA – vikki@landkrealty.com

- B.S., Engineering, University of Michigan, Ann Arbor; MBA/Finance, Arizona State University

- Vice President & CFO, Laturno Kuick Realty

- Handled and/or supervised over 300 successful short sale real estate closings in San Diego

- Worked in finance, financial planning and strategic business planning at Fortune 500 companies for 17 years

- Substantial experience investing in both the U.S. stock market and real estate

- Frequent speaker at both California and national continuing legal-education seminars